Introduction to the Psychology of Memory

Introduction to the Psychology of Memory

Michael J. A. Howe
UNIVERSITY OF EXETER
EXETER, ENGLAND

HARPER & ROW, PUBLISHERS, New York
Cambridge, Philadelphia, San Francisco,
London, Mexico City, São Paulo, Sydney

Sponsoring Editor: George Middendorf/Kathy Robinson
Project Editor: Rita Williams
Production Manager: Willie Lane
Compositor: American–Stratford Graphic Services, Inc.
Printer and Binder: R. R. Donnelley & Sons Company
Art Studio: Vantage Art, Inc.

INTRODUCTION TO THE PSYCHOLOGY OF MEMORY

Library of Congress Cataloging in Publication Data

Howe, Michael J. A., 1940–
Introduction to the psychology of memory.

Includes bibliographical references and index.
1. Memory. I. Title. [DNLM: 1. Memory. BF 371 H857ia]
BF371.H735 1983 153.1'2 82-21343
ISBN 0-06-042925-9

To the memory of my parents,
John and Mary Howe

Contents

Preface

My aim in writing this text has been to produce a short book about memory that will interest all students, not only those who have already attended an introductory psychology course. I have tried to encourage readers to think for themselves about human memory in some of the ways that scientific psychologists have done, and I attempt to demonstrate the manner in which experimental research stems from people's ideas about the nature of memory. In a short introductory volume it is permissible to be highly selective: I do not happen to think that there is a large body of knowledge that undergraduate students must acquire before they can begin to understand the psychology of memory. Nevertheless, I should point out that the present book is definitely an introduction, and makes no pretense at being more than that. Quite apart from being selective about content, I have also excluded all but the most crucial details of experimental methodology. I believe that what is most important for the beginning student is to start to think carefully and objectively about psychological questions, not to acquire a large amount of information about particular experiments, or to develop experimental skills.

When students are introduced to research in certain branches of psychology they raise pointed questions about the relevance of what they have to study to the everyday psychology of their own lives, and they find it hard to discern connections. Psychologists are sometimes justly accused of evading those psychological questions which are particularly important in the real world.

It ought to be easy to demonstrate the value and relevance of memory research. Memory is definitely crucial to everyday life. Many of the activities of daily living—understanding, learning, reasoning and solving problems, acquiring and using knowledge, finding our way from one place to another, following the many routines of ordinary life, calculating, using language and communicating with others—all share a vital dependence on our ability to keep information in memory, sometimes for no more than a few seconds, often for years. If we could not store information in memory, or gain quick access to stored information, we would quickly perish. Scientists who study the psychology of memory seek to understand the memory skills that human life depend upon: how they are operated and controlled, and how they are acquired.

In 1970, Harper & Row published my short text *Introduction to Human Memory*. It was a somewhat dry little survey of the experimental research that had been published, mainly within the previous 10 years, in the cognitive, information-processing framework that had recently proclaimed its distinctiveness from, and superiority to, the kind of verbal learning research within a broadly behaviorist tradition that was dominant in the 1950s and that remained highly active throughout the 1960s. At that time, the actual word *cognitive* was frequently waved around like a proud banner, and it took only a few more years to reach the point where some young psychologists found it hard to believe that researchers could ever have taken seriously the possibility of a noncognitive science of verbal learning and memory.

When I started working on the present text, my idea was to write an updated version of the earlier short volume. But it soon became clear that something different was needed. The direction of research into the psychology of human memory has changed a great deal since 1970. Quite apart from advances that have been made as research findings multiply, there have been major changes in the kinds of issues researchers directed their efforts toward. Perhaps the most fundamental one was the change from placing an emphasis on trying to describe the mechanisms underlying memory in terms of a series of structural elements, or stages, of a hypothetical memory system through which information is transmitted, to a desire to understand more about the kinds of processing *activities* undertaken by individuals. Such activities determine the likelihood of a person actually remembering something. Differences in these activities, together with differences in the knowledge that individuals possess, largely determine why we remember some things more accurately than others, why individuals differ at remembering various kinds of information, and why people have different rates of success at tasks that require data to be remembered. Such differences usually (but not always) favor adults compared with young children, and those people who are intelligent, or well-educated, compared with others.

In short, the shift in emphasis in memory research, from concern with the possible structure of a common memory system thought to be shared by everyone to examining the effects of activities and of differences in knowledge that individuals possess, helps to answer many important practical questions about memory that people ask themselves—and for which they look to psychologists to provide the answers. Why, for instance, do we remember A better than B, or completely forget C and retain a distorted version of D, and why is Jane generally more successful at recalling things than Jill, while Jean is noticeably poor at a variety of tasks that involve memory and Joan impressively good at remembering a wide variety of things? These questions lead to further ones, equally important, concerning the practical steps that can be taken to help those people who remember less successfully. It is these questions I attempt to address in *Introduction to the Psychology of Memory.*

Various friends and colleagues have helped to make it possible for me to write the present text, and I am grateful to all of them. I am equally indebted to the many students who have tolerated my teaching in the subject of memory and listened with patience to the sometimes oblique metaphors I introduce. Over the years I have often been supported by the friendly encouragement and guidance of George Middendorf, and to him I warmly offer my thanks. I am grateful also to Rita Williams and the editorial staff of Harper & Row, and to the anonymous reviewers who read and commented upon the initial version of the manuscript.

MICHAEL J. A. HOWE

Introduction to the Psychology of Memory

Chapter 1
Investigating Human Memory

Like most people, you probably wish you had a better memory. This book aims to describe human memory and to explain its working. Discovering how something works usually makes more effective operation possible; and important practical gains result from increased understanding of memory.

This book is based on the results of scientific investigations aimed at discovering what makes people remember. Scientists share the human desire for improved memory skills; for this and other reasons, psychologists have undertaken experimental research into human memory. I will explain some processes that cause recall of information and events. Also, I will describe a number of things people do to increase their memory's effectiveness.

THE IMPORTANCE OF REMEMBERING

You and I depend upon memory at all times, not just when we are conscious of remembering something. Memory makes a vital contribution to a wide range of circumstances where people have to retain information about various events. In almost any mental task—calculating, comprehending, thinking, or problem solving, for example—one has to retain certain essential information while the task is being performed. Take comprehension, for instance. Imagine that you listen to a sentence but do not retain the words or their meaning, forgetting each word as soon as you hear it. If that happened, you certainly would not understand the sentence you are reading now! Even a simple sentence such as "He kicked the dog" would make no sense at all. For any sentence to be comprehensible, it is essential that we retain in memory a record of the early part of the sentence ("He kicked . . .") until the remainder is heard and understood.

Memory is equally important in many other tasks we regularly perform. Try multiplying 14 × 12 in your head. Having done so, you will notice that in order to calculate you must remember the numbers. The importance of memory is indicated by the fact that we often look for ways of easing the memory load. We do so, for instance, by using paper and pencil to help us calculate a sum in arithmetic. Writing numbers down provides a permanent external memory for information. This reduces the load on a person's own internal memory.

An indication of the vital importance of memory is given by the fact that the degree of difficulty in many problem situations is largely determined by the memory demands imposed. Try to multiply 22 × 22 as a problem of mental arithmetic. It is not easy, but by no means impossible. Now imagine you are asked to multiply 222 × 222. Most people find that extremely difficult, to say the least. But ask yourself why the second calculation is so much harder than the first, and look for the differences in the two problems. In fact, the only difference is that multiplying 222 × 222, as an exercise in mental arithmetic, requires you to remember much more information than multiplying 22 × 22. Otherwise, the task requirements are remarkably simple. In each of them you simply have to know that the product of 2 × 2 = 4, and you need to be able to do simple addition.

The difficulty of many tasks depends upon the memory demands they impose. This is true in many learning, reasoning, and problem-solving situations in addition to tasks of mental calculation. For instance, you may have encountered the missionaries and cannibals problem. This problem requires discovering how a number of people (three cannibals and three missionaries) can be carried across a river in a boat that holds only two, with the constraint that there are never more cannibals than missionaries in any single place. Or you might have been asked to solve a water jar problem, requiring you to discover how one can get specified amounts of water by pouring water between jugs of different sizes. In all these problems the requirement of memorizing a shifting body of information is a major source of difficulty (Atwood & Polson, 1976).

In addition, an examination of the mental skills required in some so-called logical reasoning problems reveals that retaining appropriate information in memory is the most crucial operation. Consider the following:

1. Edith is fairer than Suzanne.
2. Edith is darker than Lili.
3. Who is the darkest?

Essentially, the route to a correct solution is to represent the items in memory as some kind of ordered list. The logical thinking necessary would be unchanged if Step 2 was removed. If one removed the second step, the problem would become extremely easy. Adding extra items does not increase the logical thought required, but it does augment the difficulty, simply because the memory load becomes greater. As in the multiplication problems above, the task is considerably simpler if one reduces the demands on memory by storing information externally—on paper, for instance. Practice at problem-solving tasks will improve your performance; it enables you to remember the steps that previously resulted in success.

A further indication of the central importance of remembering in everyday life is that doing well at memory tests is associated with high levels of achievement in many skills. For instance, people who achieve high scores on memory span tests are likely to perform well in tests of mental addition. Success at memory tests is correlated with high performance on a number of tasks used for measuring mental abilities.

In brief, there is abundant evidence that remembering and the mental processes contributing to it are vital in a wide variety of circumstances encountered in everyday life.

WHAT IS MEMORY?

When someone says "I have a bad memory" there is a suggestion that the term *memory* refers to a definite thing, rather than simply denoting a capacity to remember. But can we really locate a particular mechanism or a particular part of the brain that carries out the operations of human memory? Remembering undoubtedly does depend upon physiological processes of the brain. Yet it would be wrong to assume that the various processes in one's brain underlying the ability to remember must all be located together, or that they are entirely independent of the many other thinking and learning activities controlled by the brain. It may never be possible to point to "the memory"—to examine a particular part of the brain in the way one can examine, say, the engine in an automobile, or, indeed, the specific parts of the brain that do control activities such as vision and speech.

In the past, there was a widespread belief that the human mind consisted of a number of separate faculties, including hope, cautiousness, reason, the will, and even secretiveness and destructiveness. Memory was considered one such faculty. During the early nineteenth century would-be scientists known as *phrenologists* claimed that studying the shape of an individual's skull, and noting the positions of any bumps, indentations, or other irregularities, would make it possible to predict the relative strengths of the various mental faculties.

Such views are no longer taken seriously. There is every reason to believe that brain mechanisms making recall possible are partly inseparable from mechanisms necessary for other brain functions. Moreover, in order to answer certain practical questions like "Why is A more accurately remembered than B?," we have to refer not only to characteristics of memory in a narrow sense but also to other factors, such as mental activity occurring when an event is perceived. Relevant mental activity has an influence on the likelihood of a given thing being remembered. Nevertheless, some particular areas of the brain are essential for memory, and damage to such areas results in memory impairment. Injury to certain parts of the brain, such as the *hippocampus*, may make it impossible for a person to imprint new memories (although previously acquired knowledge may be retained). An example is the case of a man who suffered brain damage after an operation to alleviate epilepsy. Soon after the operation he moved to a new house but, after 10 weeks, had not learned his new address. He could neither find his own way home nor locate frequently used objects in the house. Each time he mowed the family lawn, for instance, he first had to ask where the lawnmower was kept; and day after day he would read the same magazine and do the same jigsaw puzzle, without any sign of recognition.

However, it is important to bear in mind that a function's being impeded by damage to a particular part of the brain does not justify concluding that the function is totally controlled by that brain area. Such a conclusion would be like surmising that, since an automobile does not operate with the spark plugs removed, the automobile's power source lies totally in the plugs. In both cases, finding that damage to one component impedes a function simply demonstrates that the component is among the (possibly numerous) contributing factors.

A person's ability to remember is not simply the outcome of a separate memory system. It is more realistic to think of memory being controlled by a number of interdependent mental processes. In one sense, memory is simply a word; one that is useful shorthand to indicate the ability to remember, but one that becomes misleading if we imagine that it refers to the mechanism that causes remembering. The fact that we use the single word *memory* need not mislead us into believing that remembering is controlled by one unitary mechanism—any more than vanity or obstinacy is controlled by distinct faculties of the human brain. Furthermore, some of the detailed processes controlling memory also contribute to other human tasks of perception, learning, and reasoning. The mental processes underlying different functions of human *cognition* (a word referring to mental skills, including learning, memory, reasoning, and thought) work together. They are by no means separate or independent from each other. As we search for ways to improve memory, we notice a practical implication of this interdependence. Some sources of improved remembering lie in perceptual processes that at first appear unrelated to memory.

THE CAUSES OF DEVELOPMENTAL CHANGES IN MEMORY

Now that we have established that processes underling human remembering are not entirely distinct or separate from processes controlling other aspects of cognition, we can start to answer some practical questions about memory. Why, (for example) does 12-year-old Sarah remember things more accurately than 6-year-old Jane? Later on, we shall examine the causes of differences in memory and the ways in which people can improve their performance. We will ask, in effect, What can Mary do to match Jack's success at remembering? For the present, I shall just make some brief observations. Neither memory improvements related to individual differences in adult ability nor improvement in children's remembering due to increasing age are caused by basic memory structures simply getting bigger or better. Improved remembering in developing children is not determined by the physiological changes that make the body muscles larger and stonger. (You may notice that a view that would expect this kind of memory development is highly implausible anyway, now that we know memory is just a useful term for abilities controlled by many different processes. But we need solid evidence to support our view.)

One piece of evidence against the belief that growth-related changes in physical structure are the main cause of the increased memory ability children exhibit as they get older is that, in some circumstances, very young infants display highly impressive memory achievements. For example, babies 6 months old can sometimes recognize pictures of faces they were shown for only a 2-minute period 2 weeks previously (Fagan, 1973). This finding suggests that the basic structures necessary for difficult recognition tasks may be largely formed by an early stage in life.

Additional evidence also contradicts the suggestion that changes in basic physical structures largely account for the developmental changes in memory. In some memory studies, young children were observed to perform just as well as adults. In one such investigation (Belmont, 1967), participants were asked to judge whether a light was brighter or dimmer than one that had been seen several seconds previously. Success at this memory task depended upon the ability to retain information about the brightness of the first light. Eight-year-old children and retarded adults performed as well on this task as normal adult people. Similarly, the results of another investigation showed that 7-year-old children were just as accurate as adults at recognizing which of two pictures, both of which had been presented earlier in a sequence of picture items, had occurred first (Brown, 1973).

Children's performance in most memory tasks, however, does improve with increasing age. Young children performing as well as adults in some tests of memory indicates that the main causes of developmental improvements do *not* lie in fundamental changes in the basic architecture of those parts of the brain controlling memory. If such fundamental developments did take place during childhood, we would expect to find very young children performing poorly on *all* memory tasks. In fact, as we have seen, this is not the case. (That is not to say, of course, that there are no physiological changes paralleling the improvements in performance we see as a child gets older.)

Where else might we find the causes of developmental improvements and individual differences in human memory? Evidence we shall introduce in later chapters indicates that differences between people in remembering are largely caused by differences in what they actually *do* in relation to materials to be remembered. These activities reflect *processes* that may be automatic or deliberate, and may be performed consciously or unconsciously. Processes undertaken with a degree of conscious deliberation are often known as *strategies* or *plans.* Some relatively complex plans for maximizing recall are called *mnemonics.* The kinds of activities people undertake at the perceptual input stage and at the later stage of attempted retrieval have a large influence upon what is remembered.

The view running through much of this text is that differences in remembering are closely related to differences in individual information processing. A person can exert a fair degree of control over some of the processing activities that influence remembering. Consequently, appropriate instruction and training may lead to large increases in what people remember. It may not be possible to devise plans and strategies that lead to improved performance in some memory tasks. The two memory tests I have just described, where young children performed as well as adults, provide possible examples. Also, it is possible that when presented with an unfamiliar task, one may not be able to select or devise an appropriate strategy immediately. However, in most circumstances, activities individuals undertake *will* affect remembering.

A large number of mental processes influence human memory. Mental processes are unobservable, and their presence can only be *inferred* through ingenious experimental research. But one's observable activities are related to one's underlying mental processes, and can be measured and manipulated. A large number of different activities individuals undertake as they receive information and events have measurable effects upon their recall.

The activities individuals perform are by no means the only factors that influence memory. The individual's existing knowledge about what is being perceived is particularly important. The ways one's existing knowledge contributes to one's remembering events will be explored in later chapters.

AN ANALOGY

In these pages we have already tried to answer the question "What is memory like?" or "What kind of a phenomenon is memory?" A crude analogy can be illuminating provided we do not push it too far. Think of two people's memories as being like two vegetable gardens, in plots of identical size, with identical soil. The basic structure of the two gardens is thus identical, but the two may be far from identical in what they actually produce. Structural size places some limits on output; however, the achievements of the two gardens may differ enormously nonetheless. The source of the difference lies not in structure, but in the work done by those who cultivate the gardens—those who design them, decide what to sow and when, and so on.

Thus, the achievements of each garden depend to a large extent on how the basic plots are cultivated, and not simply on their size or composition. Similarly, with memory, what a person actually remembers after perceiving some information or event will depend on how the information is processed. The processes that underlie one's activities are as important as the basic architecture of the memory system. Whenever one individual remembers things more accurately than another person, the cause of the difference may lie in processing activities rather than in basic memory structure.

Alternative analogies could be introduced to make the same point. For example, differences in people's ability to remember are in some respects like differences in two computers with identical basic elements but different programming. Each has the same capacity for performing tasks, but their actual achievements are by no means identical. The student who is good at remembering his lecture notes might be someone whose brain is simply well programmed to perform memory tasks.

We must be wary, however, about analogies introduced to help understand memory. Human memory is in many important respects entirely different from garden plots, or computers, or any other phenomena sharing some of memory's characteristics. Beyond a certain point, we can only answer the question What is memory like? by admitting that human memory is like nothing except itself.

THE ANCIENT ART OF REMEMBERING

To the modern mind, it is a commonplace that it is useful to find out how something works if we want to make it operate better. We take it for granted that the most efficient way to improve memory is to gain a better understanding of its workings. People in ancient times were just as anxious to improve recall, but the idea that increased scientific knowledge provided the best route to practical advances was outside their experience. When they sought ways to increase remembering they gave little attention to understanding how memory actually operates. They were interested in the *art* of memory: They did not share our concern with the *science* of explaining remembering. Nevertheless, their practical efforts were highly successful. A number of effective memory aids, known as *mnemonics,* were produced. The following technique, known as the place method, provides a good example.

The Roman orator Cicero wrote that the place method was discovered about 2,500 years ago by a Greek poet named Simonides. According to Cicero, Simonides was called away from a banquet where he had been reciting a poem by a messenger of the gods Castor and Pollux, who were praised in the poem. While he was outside the banquet hall the roof collapsed, killing everyone inside. The bodies were so mangled that they were unrecognizable. However, Simonides was able to identify each body by its location in the building.

As you can see from this story, one applies the place method (also known as the method of loci) by forming a visual image of the items to be remembered and linking each image with a highly familiar location. In order to recall the items, one simply evokes the image of the location, thereby retrieving the accompanying item image.

Try the method for yourself. It may help you remember a list of items you must purchase. Use locations that are thoroughly familiar, such as the rooms of your own home. Give yourself at least 5 seconds to form a clear visual image of each of the items you wish to remember, situated in a particular place. When you want to recall the list, simply revisit, in your mind's eye, the familiar home locations.

Individuals differ in the ease with which they form visual images, but most people find the place method an effective way to remember a list of separate items. In Chapter 5 I shall have more to say about the recall functions of imagery.

The mnemonics invented in the distant past were useful for tasks important at the time. The place method, for instance, was used by orators to help recall the different topics to be covered in a speech. (*Topic* is derived from the Greek word *topos*, meaning place.) Some of the mnemonics devised in the past are little used today, either because the tasks they were formed to aid are now uncommon, or because alternative aids to memory are preferred.

We now often rely upon external memory aids, such as paper and pencil, rather than the internal memory aids provided by mnemonic devices. As I remarked earlier, computing 222 × 222 is much easier when performed with a pencil and paper than when performed by mental arithmetic. Writing is a particularly common external memory aid. In fact, most of the external memory aids used today depend upon literacy, although nonliterate people do possess various memory aids of their own. For example, Australian aborigines make use of carefully notched sticks to prompt memory when delivering complicated messages that must be retained over a long period of time (Hunter, 1979).

Mnemonic aids are common in everyday life. Few English-speaking people could say how many days there are in the month of March if they did not know a rhyme mnemonic such as the one beginning "Thirty days hath September. . . ." Many individuals depend upon a first-letter mnemonic to help them recall the colors of the rainbow: "Richard Of York Gave Battle In Vain," or "red, orange, yellow, green, blue, indigo, violet." Similar memory aids are used to remember the names of the planets, in order of distance from the sun.

We shall encounter a number of mnemonics in later chapters. As I have indicated, mnemonic systems were first produced for practical reasons, drawing upon a tradition of an art of memory not based upon scientific explanation. Until recently, psychologists interested in scientific investigations of memory took little notice of mnemonics. They were regarded simply as tricks used by stage performers and by authors of books with sensational titles such as *Give Yourself a Superpower Memory*. It was felt they had little to offer science. Mnemonics and those promoting their use were thought to be slightly disreputable. Eventually, however, psychologists realized that some of the systems were effective and deserved psychological study. In particular, the study of mnemonics helped draw attention to the importance of various activities people undertake while attempting to remember, particularly the forming of visual images.

Chapter 2
How Does Memory Work?

"In one ear and out the other!" cries a frustrated mother at her youngest son's most recent memory lapse. The implication that memory has a physical location in the brain, somewhere between the two ears, does not greatly help us to understand human memory, but it is at least a start.

How does memory work and how can we begin to discover how it works? One basic way to find out how an item operates is to consider similar things that are more familiar, possibly simpler, and *already* explainable. This procedure may at least give us some useful hints.

MEMORY AS A STORE

Storage is the most obvious function of memory. How is storage achieved? Consider a very simple mechanism for storing physical items.

Imagine that you need to put away some winter clothes. You may decide to keep them in a chest of drawers, which provides storage. When you have some clothes that need to be safely stored, you simply put them into the drawer (input). Once there, they will remain in the drawer (retention) until you need them. At that point, all you have to do is to take out the item you need (retrieval). If the number of clothes to be packed away exceeds the drawer's capacity, you can either look for a larger drawer or use more than one.

This simple account of the way a drawer is used can serve as a possible explanation, or theory, of how information is retained in human memory. It makes provision for the entry or *input* of items into the memory store, for their *retention,* and for their removal or *retrieval* when required. All these functions are also necessary for human recall.

An adequate theory of memory is one that can explain everything known about remembering. If the drawer theory of memory achieved this, there would be no need for further research or more sophisticated explanations. However, as you might expect, the drawer theory is by no means adequate: There are too many facts it does not explain. When we gain detailed knowledge about the actual functions of human memory—what memory achieves, and what its limitations are—we will produce another hypothesis, one accounting for aspects of human memory the drawer theory does not satisfactorily explain.

In the following pages, we shall learn some facts about memory phenomena demonstrating that they are different from the processes adequate for storing clothes in a drawer. Most of the evidence comes from psychological finding gleaned from experiments. However, we can start with a commonsense observation. We use drawers to store items in relatively small numbers, but the human memory must retain millions of items. We can increase the number of items that a drawer can store by enlarging its size. But imagine that you have a drawer that really does contain a million separate pieces of clothing. It would have to be very strong and somewhat gigantic. Yet there is no fundamental reason why such a drawer could not be constructed. All items would be safely retained once in the drawer; the drawer would perform its storage function without fault. But what would happen when you needed to use one particular shirt, say, from among the million retained in the drawer? Now you have a real problem! The one you want is safely stored, but finding it among the hundreds of others, most of them resembling the one you are looking for, will be quite a headache. It is very likely you will need to look through 500,000, or half of the million, before you find the one you want. Let's assume that the searching speed is one second per item scanned.

In that case, finding the sought item would take exactly 500,000 seconds, which is more than 800 hours! Clearly, the system is beginning to look less than adequate; and a human memory system working along these lines would be no use at all.

This example introduces an important necessary attribute human memory has in common with any large storage system. Not only must all items be safely stored, they must be retained in such a way that one can be readily located when it is needed. The system must be designed to ensure ready access to the items stored there. In human memory, access is accomplished by processes taking place both at the input stage (initial perception) and at the retrieval stage (later recall). Some of these processes will be discussed in later chapters.

EXPERIMENTS AND EXPLANATIONS

In order to investigate the workings of memory, psychologists undertake experiments: People's performance at tasks making demands upon memory is measured under carefully controlled circumstances. In some instances, scientific progress follows a neat sequence of research activities: Explanatory theories are advanced, tested in experimental research, and subsequently refined and retested. Eventually, scientists arrive at a theory accounting for all known facts, and the theory is then regarded as a satisfactory explanation.

Progress toward increased understanding of human memory, however, has not been nearly as straightforward as the above model. The relationship between theoretical explanations and experimental investigations has not been at all clear-cut. Furthermore, in psychology and in other sciences, an explanation is sometimes challenged or abandoned not simply because it is found to be incorrect, but because scientists become convinced that a different approach is needed (Kuhn, 1962). (Something of this kind happened in the field of memory research in the early 1970s. Investigations shifted emphasis: Scientists went from trying to specify the structure or architecture of human memory to determining which active functions and processes influence what is remembered.)

Returning to our earlier attempt to explain memory, we find research yields a number of findings about human memory that cannot be explained by the drawer-for-storing-clothes theory. Consider, for example, what happens when we overload memory—when more items are presented within a short period than can be remembered. We may ask people to hear lists of unrelated words, presented at a rate of one per second. If we then ask for recall of the items, we will find that perfect performance occurs only if the lists are relatively short, containing not more than eight or nine words. The maximum number of words a person can recall after one presentation without error is known as the *memory span.* It does not depend greatly upon the particular items: They can be digits, letters, numbers, or nonsense syllables.

Predictions of the Drawer Theory

What happens when the number of items presented is greater than one's memory span? According to the drawer theory, there are a number of

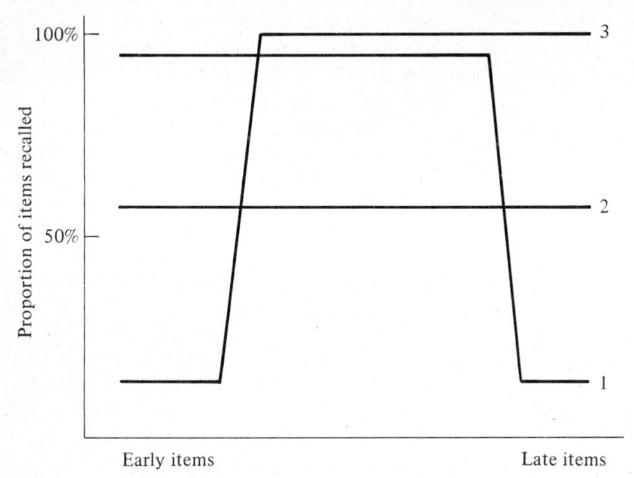

Figure 2.1 Possible memory outcomes of the drawer theory.

possible outcomes, some of which are depicted in Figure 2.1. The first possibility, shown by line 1 in Figure 2.1, is that the drawer will suddenly become full, and no further items will be accepted. Translated to memory, this means the early items would be recalled perfectly. But later items, once the span was exceeded, would not be remembered at all. A second possibility (line 2 in Figure 2.1) is that stored information might be squeezed or distorted with the addition of more items. The probability of recalling each item might be depressed. A third possibility, depicted by line 3, assumes that the drawer is backless: As new items enter the full drawer, the earlier items are displaced. Therefore, the most recent items, up to the number in the memory span, will be remembered. The earlier ones will be forgotten.

The next step is to explore what actually happens when memory span is exceeded, and to note which (if any) of the predictions the drawer theory generates match the findings. Jahnke (1963) performed an experiment presenting lists containing five to nine consonants, and then asked people to recall the consonants. His results are shown in Figure 2.2. It shows similar result patterns with a variety of list lengths: As length exceeds memory span, it is the items around the middle of a list that suffer. The earliest and latest items are recalled comparatively well.

It is quite clear that the findings of Jahnke's experiment do not match any of the predictions our simple drawer theory indicates. Furthermore (and it is hard to think of any way the theory could be modified to predict the experimental findings that actually occurred), the drawer theory failed an important test: It did not generate any predictions that matched reality. The hard evidence requires an alternative explanation.

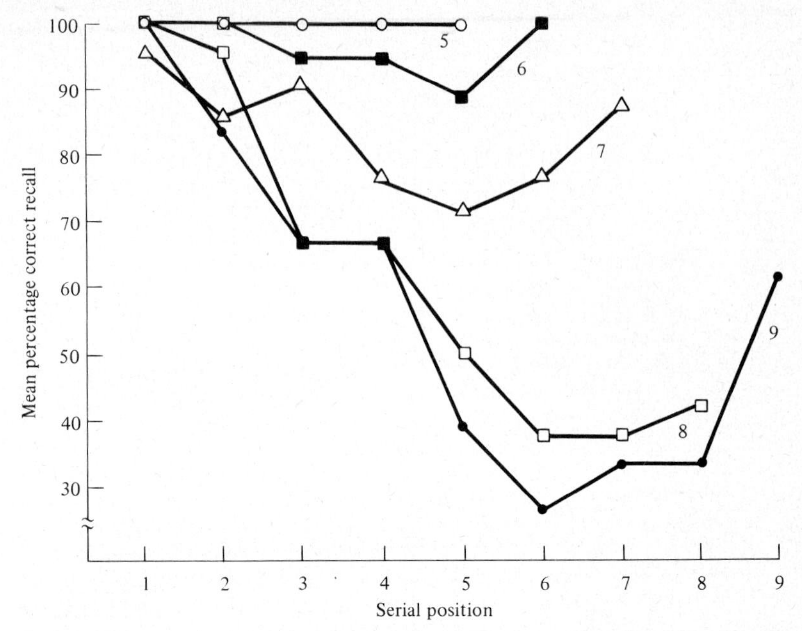

Figure 2.2 Serial position curves for lists of consonants. *Source:* Jahnke (1963).

Jahnke's results demonstrate that adults do not remember all events equally well. In fact, this is a common finding, and it is one that any satisfactory memory theory must at least attempt to explain. Most people are aware that some things are better remembered than others, and there is ample experimental evidence to confirm this impression. It has been found, for instance, that people inspecting a list of nine letters, presented at a rate of one per second, then most easily recall items occurring towards the end of the sequence (Howe, 1965). The early letters are recalled with considerably less accuracy. However, if recall is delayed for a few seconds, the items occurring early in the list are better remembered than the later items.

A number of factors contribute to this apparently strange result. Most probably, by the time presentation of the list is completed, some of the early letters have been forgotten, and the late items are not. This explains the finding that the later items are the ones most accurately reproduced when recall is requested immediately after presentation. On the other hand, memory for the remembered early items may be relatively fixed, consolidated in a person's memory, perhaps as a result of the letters at the beginning of a list being rehearsed for a longer period of time than the later items.

Whatever the precise explanation, it is important to note that, even within a few seconds' time span, there are large differences in both the accuracy of a subject's ability to recall events and the extent that items become consolidated in memory. An adequate explanation of memory must be able to account for findings like these. A more complex account of memory than the primitive drawer theory will almost certainly be necessary.

STRUCTURAL THEORIES OF MEMORY

In the late 1950s, progress occurred in explaining the workings of memory. Some explanatory theories, in the form of simple diagrams describing memory and attention phenomena, were published. The explanations were generally precise enough to be tested empirically. Thus, they could be verified or contradicted by careful experimental research. Most of the attempts to explain memory concentrated on showing how human memory systems dealt with materials needing to be retained over fairly short periods of time.

A British experimental psychologist, Donald Broadbent, proposed that human memory operated along the principles indicated in Figure 2.3. It is not entirely unlike the drawer theory already discussed, but it is considerably more complicated. It contains a number of separate stages for data storage, and also contains provisions for processes such as information filtering. In the course of some investigations into human attention and speech perception, Broadbent noticed that people were unable to attend simultaneously to a number of separate messages. We are often exposed to a number of different sources of information, but cannot process them all at the same time. In these circumstances, it is necessary to attend selectively to some events; others are shut out. This poses a problem. How do we avoid losing the unattended message, which might be highly important? A mechanism that briefly retains, or holds, informa-

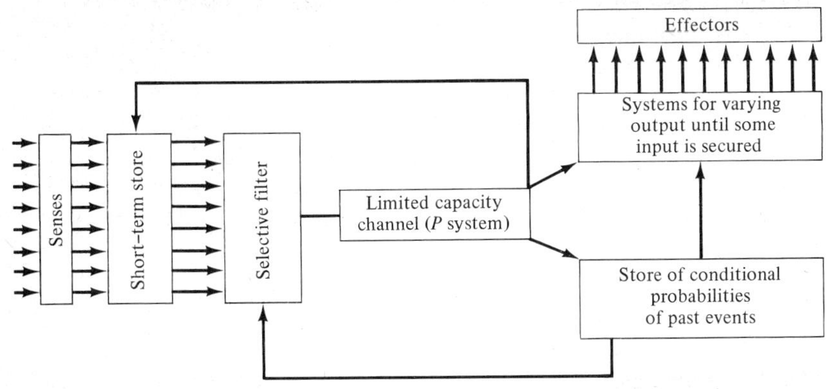

Figure 2.3 Broadbent's flow diagram for newly perceived information. *Source:* Broadbent (1958).

tion not attended to during the time we attend to the processing of other information might be a solution. Information briefly retained in the holding mechanism might then be processed as soon as the necessary capacity became available.

The data from Broadbent's experimental investigations suggested to him that human memory does indeed possess functions of this kind. Accordingly, he hypothesized that incoming information is first held in a temporary short-term store, as depicted in Figure 2.3. The information then arrives at the selection filter; this in turn is tuned to direct certain kinds of messages for further processing. Information that is *not* selected at this stage is liable to decay fairly rapidly. Alternatively, it may pass through the limited capacity channel depicted in the figure and return to the temporary store, where it may be retained for a few seconds longer.

Broadbent's explanation draws attention to the close relationships existing between perceiving, attending, and remembering. The notion of a selective filter introduces a number of problems that need not concern us at the moment. However, some parts of Broadbent's account, primarily the idea that human memory possesses mechanisms to hold some information until it is attended to and processed, are widely accepted.

Stages

A number of other descriptions or models of memory were subsequently developed. These are known as *stage models* because, like Broadbent's account, they depict memory as a series of subsystems in which information transmits from one part or stage to another. Most of the stage models are in some respects similar to Broadbent's. Typically, these models indicate that, as one perceives new information inputs detected by the sensory receptors, the new input may be temporarily retained in a relatively unprocessed form. This new information is kept in what are sometimes known as *peripheral stores.* Afterwards, according to most stage models of human memory, information may be retained in a *short-term* or *active* memory store. This has contents roughly corresponding to those of conscious awareness. Information may remain in the short-term store for up to a few seconds; the period of time may be extended by the recirculation of information into the store.

This process may necessitate active rehearsal. Some of the information receives more extensive processing, enabling it to be retained relatively permanently—in the *long-term* store. The latter contains a large body of information sufficiently processed and analyzed to be retained for lengthy periods. It is retrievable when necessary. In general, long-term memory retains some representation of the meaning of the information. Most stage models, despite the attention paid to the need for multiple stores, have relatively little to say about the detailed attributes of long-term retention.

The stage theories of memory developed in the 1960s aimed to describe in outline the operations of human memory in terms of data transmission between different analytical and storage stages. To varying extents, stage theory authors hypothesized that the different stages should correspond to the actual structure of the human memory system, at least as far as short-term memory was concerned.

The psychologists developing these ideas were influenced by knowledge of computer systems that performed some functions similar to those of human memory. In order to do difficult tasks, a computer, like a human brain, has to retain large amounts of information and must quickly locate the information when it is needed. Information has to be transferred between various points within the computer system, and several memory stores having different functions may be required. Researchers who were trying to discover how human memory works found a knowledge of the functioning of artificial computer memory systems helpful in providing suggestions about possible mechanisms underlying the operation of adult memory. Consequently, the stage theories of memory displayed the imprint of ideas from computer science. Of course, in many ways humans are *not* like computers: Suggestions based on knowledge of memory in computers can be misleading as well as helpful.

PROCESSING

Stage theories have been very influential. They have helped psychologists discover how human memory systems operate. However, in recent years, the emphasis on attempting to describe memory in terms of stages representing the architecture or structure of human memory has been replaced. The emphasis now is on a different (but not unrelated) memory influence: That is, the way that people actively *process* events perceived.

There are several reasons for the diminished interest in stage theories. It may, for example, be quite simply wrong to assume separate memory stores exist. There are other ways to account for the fact that not all items are remembered equally well. Having separate stores is uneconomical in some respects, and might make the job of locating retained information unnecessarily difficult.

Also stage theories are not very helpful in answering practical questions about memory. They do not tell us why Jane remembers the wedding anniversary her husband forgets, or why Professor Jones can never remember his students' names. When someone asks why we can retain some kinds of knowledge more easily than other kinds, or why Jane is better at remembering than Jack, stage theories do not give useful answers. We do not find that differences in the structural aspects of memory emphasized in stage theories provide the explanation for differences in what people actually remember.

On the other hand, explanations stressing differences in the ways people process information *do* account for differences in remembering. Knowledge about processing can help us explain why some people remember more than others. We can use this knowledge in order to help people remember things with greater success. Furthermore, developmental differences in children's and adults' memory abilities are also caused, in part, by differences in mental processing. In short, placing more stress on memory processing and less on memory structure may make it easier to answer practical questions concerning recall, and to find ways to increase what people actually remember.

REPRESENTING EVENTS IN MEMORY

In spite of the objections to the view that there are physically separate stages in memory (a view not held by all stage theorists), no one questions the value of drawing attention to the separate and distinct *functions* of memory. Most importantly, information is held in memory through different means. To be more precise, memory retains *representations* of events and the representations (or *descriptions*) held in memory can be of various aspects of a perceived event: its appearance, sound, or meaning. The representation is formed and stored in memory as a result of processing taking place while the event is perceived. The input is thus analyzed while being perceived. In general, extracting the meaning of an event necessitates more extensive processing than simple detection does. However, those events more extensively processed are correspondingly more likely to be remembered, because their memory representations are more durable, or more accessible at the time of retrieval, or both.

Brief Visual Storage

The ideas summarized in the previous paragraph will be developed in a more leisurely fashion in later chapters. For the present, the essential thing to understand is that human memory retains representations describing different aspects of perceived events. First, let us look at some evidence indicating that people retain a visual record, in the form of a literal copy of the perceived event, for very short periods. As I remarked earlier, the brain may have holding mechanisms retaining information for brief periods—for instance, while data is waiting to be processed.

Some experiments by George Sperling (1963) demonstrated that people can briefly retain a visual record of what they perceive. Sperling asked people to look at visual displays containing 12 letters in 3 rows of 4 letters each. The displays were presented for periods of less than a second, using an apparatus known as a *tachistoscope.* The subjects knew in advance they would be required to recall the letters in just one of the three rows. That row would be designated by sounding one of three auditory tones just after the visual display had disappeared.

Sperling wanted to discover what was stored in memory during the fraction of a second after the display finished. He did not ask for recall of all the letters (as experiments in memory-span tests normally do) to avoid the distortion caused by the forgetting during the period of item recall. By requiring only a sample of the items, he was able to minimize this. Therefore, recall of the 4 sample items provided a good measure of what was actually *available* in memory at the moment the recall request was given. Since subjects did not know in advance which of the 3 rows would be required, it was assumed that the average proportion of each 4-letter row recalled provided an accurate indication of the proportion of the entire 12-letter array available in memory. Thus, if a subject always recalled all 4 of the requested letters, Sperling deduced that, at the moment the tone sounded, all 12 of the items in the display were available in memory.

Using this sampling method, Sperling found that people were able to recall around two-thirds of the letters if the time interval between the disappearance of the display and the signal designating the row of letters required was about a tenth of a second. This represents a memory span of 8 or 9 items, considerably better than the score obtained when all 12 items are required in otherwise identical (brief visual presentation) conditions. In that event, only about 4.5 of the 12 items are recalled, on the average.

Sperling's findings demonstrate a capacity for brief visual retention of perceived items over brief periods of time, normally under a second. The information thus retained may be a fairly literal copy of the visual display. This record seems to demand a relatively small amount of processing, requiring little time. (Producing such a record most probably does not involve the extensive processing needed in order to provide a description or representation of a perceived event designating its meaning. In the latter case, it is necessary to analyze the newly perceived event in relation to a person's knowledge. This involves considerably more extensive, and probably more time-consuming, processing.)

Sperling's research drew attention to the human capacity to briefly retain a visual record of newly perceived events, without extensive mental processing. This capacity has been termed *peripheral memory* by some writers, to indicate the (perhaps unjustified) belief that the limited processing necessary is achieved by perceptual coding mechanisms adjoining the sensory receptors. This processing may not involve all of the memory mechanisms used when information is more extensively analyzed. Other writers prefer the term *iconic memory.* The brief visual storage mechanism usefully keeps materials temporarily available during processing operations. If the analysis necessary for providing more permanent representations of items takes any appreciable time, or if there is the slightest delay at any point, it is essential to have a way to keep materials briefly available. The mechanism Sperling demonstrated makes this possible.

Brief Auditory Retention

A related discovery was that descriptions of *auditory* characteristics are retained in memory. Information may remain available in aural form for at least several seconds. Evidence about human memory holding descriptions of auditory characteristics of events was obtained by R. Conrad (1962, 1964). He asked people to listen to letter sequences, having first made sure his subjects had no difficulties hearing the letters, and he subsequently asked for recall.

Conrad then inspected the mistakes his subjects made and found that, when an incorrect letter was recalled, it was frequently one *sounding like* the correct one. For example, a subject might say *t* or *d* when the correct letter was *b*.

The results of this study indicate auditory factor involvement at some stage in memory. Imagine that the following descriptions are temporarily retained in memory:

the sound of *b*
the sound of *t*
the sound of *d*
the sound of *f*

Some forgetting occurs, so the memory record becomes imperfect. If partial loss of the auditory recordings of *b*, *t* and *d* occurs, these items may cease to be discernable, since memory can auditorily discriminate only if the sound record is relatively complete. However, it is possible to discriminate *d* and *f* from each other even if a large auditory portion of each is lost.

Conrad found the pattern of recall errors where one letter was substituted for another surprisingly similar to the pattern of hearing errors found when conditions for hearing are poor, causing letters that sound alike to become confused. However, there was no doubt that subjects in the recall experiment had initially heard the letters correctly. In fact, similar errors are found even when letters are presented visually instead of aurally. Therefore, the "hearing errors" must occur at a later stage, after the items enter memory.

This finding suggests that some memory retention is a record of the sounds (or possibly the articulatory aspects) of letters. (Also note that, if any information about the *visual* qualities of the letters is retained, we would expect some recall errors to take the form of visual confusion: for example, *o* instead of *c*. As it happens, errors of this kind are very rare.)

ACTIVE MEMORY

An important contribution of stage theories is to draw attention to the need for a highly accessible short-term memory store. Obviously, people must retain vast quantities of information, related to many kinds of knowledge. But it is also necessary to have some kind of *active* memory system for dealing with data currently in use. For instance, to mentally multiply 22×22 it is essential to possess the knowledge (in long-term memory) that $2 \times 2 = 4$, $4 + 4 = 8$, and so on. It is also essential to have the means to temporarily store those numbers being held and manipulated during the period of time the multiplication task is actually being performed.

Terms such as *short-term memory, active memory* and *working memory* are used in this context. Broadly speaking, these functions correspond to "what a person is conscious of remembering" at a particular moment. External data may enter the active memory directly, and it may or may not be subsequently retained on a relatively permanent basis. Alternatively, information from a person's own long-term knowledge may enter active memory. This happens, for example, when someone makes use of existing knowledge (for example, "$2 + 2 = 4$") in order to perform a current task. The number of unrelated items that can simultaneously be held in active memory is strictly limited to around seven separate items, according to George Miller (1956). This number broadly corresponds to the size of the memory span.

Items are typically retained in active memory for periods of less than a minute. This amount of time may be as long as the items are needed. Subsequently, any of three possible chains of events may take place. First, items in active memory but not also in a long-term store may be lost from memory, either through a decay process or through their simply becoming inaccessible. Figure 2.4 shows the results of an experiment by Peterson and Peterson (1959), in which students tried to recall consonants they had heard but were prevented from rehearsing because they had been given an extra task (counting). The rapid decline in recall shows that unrehearsed items in short-term memory that do not receive further processing or special attention quickly become unavailable. It is not entirely clear precisely what happens to them. (A stored item may be inaccessible simply because its description is not sufficiently precise to enable its location among a large number of indiscriminable stored items. This will be explained more fully in Chapter 3.)

The second chain of events may be that briefly retained items re-

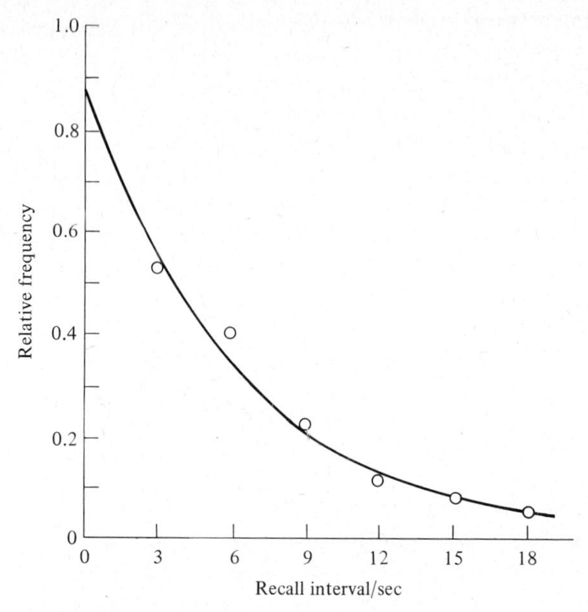

Figure 2.4 Effects of interval on recall of syllables. *Source:* Peterson and Peterson (1959).

ceive further processing, resulting in a permanently available representation. Third, an item may be recirculated into the temporary system, through rehearsal or some related activity. Consequently, the item may be maintained in active memory longer than it would remain under other circumstances. In practical outcome, this may make it possible to perform a task: for example, keeping a telephone number through rehearsal until it is dialed. Alternatively, recirculation may provide further processing opportunities, possibly leading to a permanent representation in storage.

Available processing capacity for active memory is limited. And this capacity is partly shared by other important functions—such as attention—as Broadbent's model in Figure 2.3 (p. 15) indicates. Consequently, the greater the amount of processing required for active memory at a given time, the less is available for other current tasks, and vice versa. An experiment by Baddeley and Hitch (1974) explored increasing the amount of material people were instructed to keep in active memory while listening to passages of information in prose form at the same time. The experimenters found that retaining six digits in memory significantly reduced subjects' comprehension of the passages read to them.

As I explained, stage theories have in recent years lost some of their impetus for driving research. The structure of human memory inevitably limits what people can actually remember. But performance is not only determined by structure, and the memory differences that seem practically important are explained primarily by differences in processes rather than in structures. Of course, an interest in multistore stage theories need not lead to processes' neglect, and some stage models considerably emphasize the importance of control processes. Nevertheless, there has been a shift in memory research: Increased attention is given to people's active memory processes. This change has important implications. As we will see in the following chapters, an emphasis on active processes is helpful in trying to answer practical questions about why some things are remembered and others forgotten, about why some people remember more than others, about why adult memory differs from children's, and about what can be done to increase memory ability.

Chapter 3
Processing and Remembering

INPUT PROCESSING

I can remember things that happened when I was 3 years old, but I have no recollection of shaving this morning.

Some events are remembered very clearly: Others are quickly forgotten. Why is this? In the present chapter we introduce an important cause of differences. We can start by describing a simple experiment.

College students enrolled in a course on learning and memory were told to look at words displayed on a screen in their regular classroom. Each word appeared for 1 second; 5 seconds later the next word appeared. Every student looked at 60 words in all. Previously, the students had been given booklets containing 60 questions, 1 for each of the words displayed. The procedure was to look at a question just before the word was shown and then answer the question as soon as it appeared. There were three kinds of questions. On half the occasions the right answer was "yes"; "no" was correct on the others.

One type of question concerned the physical structure of the word about to be displayed: It asked about the *case* of the word. Students were asked "Is the word in capital letters?" The word subsequently appearing might, for example, be *TABLE,* making the correct answer "yes." Alternatively, the word might be *table,* making the answer "no."

Questions in the second category inquired about the *phonemic quality* (that is, the *sound*) of the word shown. These questions asked if the word rhymed with a particular item. For example, one question asked "Does the word rhyme with *weight?*" If the word was *crate,* the correct answer was "yes," but if it was, say, *market,* the answer was "no."

Finally, questions of a third type asked about the *meanings* (known as the *semantic* attributes) of the words. These questions related to the word's semantic (meaningful) category. For example, when the word was *copper,* the question might be "Is the word a metal?" The correct answer would be "yes," but "Is the word a kind of fruit?" would require a "no."

Thus the three different types of question required students to attend either to the physical (visual) structure of the word, to the sound of the word, or to the meaning of the word. Every student received 20 questions of each kind, and every participant looked at the same words (but in different orders to avoid a possible source of experimental bias). The reason for undertaking the study was to discover if the mental activities students performed in order to answer the questions had any effect upon memory of the words. The experimenters (Craik & Tulving, 1975) thought that the different types of questions would lead to different aspects of words being mentally analyzed and processed.

After the students worked their way through all 60 words, they were given a surprise memory test to find out how many words they recognized. The recognition test materials consisted of a list containing 180 words. Sixty of these words, randomly distributed among the others, were the items that had previously been displayed. The students' task was to identify these particular words.

The findings of the investigation show (as do those of a number of similar experiments, for example, that of Tresselt & Mayzner, 1960) that the kind of question preceding a word item, and hence the type of analysis a person undertakes, has a large influence on the probability of that word's being recognized. The percentage of items correctly recognized following the three different kinds of questions were as follows:

Structure questions ("In capitals?")	26% recognized
Phonemic questions ("Does it rhyme with . . . ?)	46% recognized
Semantic category questions ("Is it a metal?")	72% recognized

Note the sheer size of the recall differences, despite the fact that in each case students saw the words for an identical amount of time. The mental activities students performed while inspecting the words in order to answer the questions had an enormous influence upon the word's being remembered. That is, the mental processing activity taking place during perception was a major cause of remembering.

In short, the experiment's findings indicate that the likelihood of an event being remembered is related to the mental processing occurring when a person perceives it. The retained information, known as a *memory trace*, takes the form of a representation or description of some aspect(s) of the perceived event.

A restricted analysis, making limited demands upon a person's mental processing capacity, leads to the production of a stored memory trace describing the physical structure of an item: one specifying its sensory features, such as size, shape, color, pitch, or loudness.

Remember that the term memory trace refers to the actual representation or description stored in memory. The analysis taking place when events are perceived produces memory traces that can describe events in terms of these physical qualities (Jacoby, Craik, & Begg, 1979).

Levels of Processing

The perceptual analysis of an item achieved by mental processing at the time of input may be relatively crude and simple, or it may be more extensive. According to Craik and Lockhart (1972) and Cermak (1972), separate processing levels are involved. According to Cermak:

> Information could be conceived of as passing through. . . . stages of encoding. . . . at the same time that the acoustic properties of a word are becoming well-established, a weak semantic encoding can be starting. The word passes through various stages of encoding, being categorized more and more specifically. (Cermak, 1972, p. 258)

Craik and Lockhart present a similar view:

> The memory trace can be understood as a by-product of perceptual analysis and. . . . trace persistence is a positive function of the depth to which the stimulus has been analyzed. (Craik & Lockhart, 1972, p. 671)

They also state:

> Analysis proceeds through a series of sensory stages to levels associated with matching or pattern recognition and finally to semantic-associative stages of stimulus enrichment. . . . One of the results of this perceptual analysis is the memory trace. . . . trace persistence is a function of depth of analysis, with deeper levels of analysis associated with more elaborate, longer lasting, and stronger traces. (Craik & Lockhart, 1972, p. 675)

To form a memory trace that describes an event in terms of its meaning, further mental processing is required. The perceptual analysis necessary for describing an event's meaning (or its abstracted attributes) involves not just the physical form of the input but also requires matches or comparisons being made between the newly perceived event and knowledge already sorted in one's memory. The more elaborate analysis, which is said by Craik and Lockhart to involve greater depth of processing, leads to the formation of memory traces describing items in terms of their meaningful attributes.

The participants in the study by Craik and Tulving were made to process the items they perceived by having to answer different kinds of questions about the items. However, giving people questions to answer is by no means the only way to control input processing. In a number of studies by J. J. Jenkins (for example, in Hyde & Jenkins, 1969), people were asked to perform different tasks on newly perceived items. This included counting the number of syllables, detecting particular letters, or rating words on the basis of their degree of importance or pleasantness. In general, his experimental findings closely parallel those of Craik and Tulving. When the task requires subjects to consider items' meaning, subsequent recall is much more accurate than when the task only demands attention to the physical structure of words.

Returning briefly to the experimental results, we recall that the questions requiring students to process the meaning of a word led to far more recognition than the other questions. For practical purposes, if we want to help Jane Doe remember something, a good plan is to give her a task that leads to processing the to-be-remembered information in a meaningful way. For reasons I will discuss later, memory traces describing an event in terms of its meaning are generally much more effective in ensuring recall than memory traces describing only physical attributes.

THE CONCEPT OF PROCESSING

It is time to be a little more precise about what we mean by processing. First, consider the memory representation that mental processing activities achieve. A system storing information about an *event* (we can use this term to refer to any identifiable item or happening) retains some record or representation describing the event. However, the precise form of the representation varies. Imagine, for example, that you want to record a rock concert. You could do this by recording on magnetic tape, or on a phonograph record, or by using an optical form of recording, such as 35 mm film. In each case the required information is retained (as we discover when we reproduce the sound), but the three alternative systems store the information in quite different ways.

Note that unless you have appropriate reproducing equipment, there is no easy way to identify what is stored on tape, film, or disc. Similarly, when information necessary for performing a task is stored in a computer, the information is first transformed into a particular form (computer language) appropriate for the computer's operation. A human observer finds nothing in the computer store that can be readily identified as relating to the information in it. In human memory there is similar uncertainty concerning precisely how an item is stored. If I can remember, say, the number 9, all that can be said with certainty about the storage of that number in my memory is my brain must have retained some description of the number, or information about it, in a form compatible with the brain's systems for processing and computing information.

Processing and Stored Descriptions

According to the explanation advanced by Craik and Lockhart (1972), different levels of processing are necessary for the perceptual analyses that transform (or *encode*) information about the various items' attributes into forms stored as memory traces. Thinking about a concrete example makes it easier to understand this. Imagine that you have to make an artificial memory to store information about a small collection of books. The purpose of the memory (or catalog) is to make it possible for you to identify each book and quickly locate any particular one you want.

What kind of information about the books might the memory retain? One possibility is simply to record the *number of pages* in each book. Doing so would not be unlike undertaking the relatively superficial processing that occurs when one perceives the physical attributes of an item and retains a corresponding memory trace. You thus obtain a description of each book, based on the number of pages it contains. So long as the number of books is fairly small, having a record of the number of pages in each enables you to identify any particular book needed. In short, specifying the number of pages in a book provides an adequate description of that particular item, making it possible to identify it.

But if the collection of books is large, stored descriptions simply detailing the number of pages in each will be less effective for locating a particular volume. There might be several books with the same number of pages. In that case, the stored information would be inadequate for uniquely identifying one particular book. In order to specify particular books within a large collection, it is essential to have descriptions that are more precise.

One way to describe a book precisely is to say something about its contents: for example, "It's about interpreting dreams." But—and this is important—note that the amount of active processing you must do in order to register the meaningful content of a book is much greater than necessary for simply counting the number of pages. (If you doubt this, pile a stack of books in front of you and try doing it for yourself!) As a rule, if the library is a large one, the book descriptions that you can achieve by simple measurement processes such as counting the pages, or recording the weight, size, or color of each item, are unlikely to be as useful for finding one book among many than the more precise descriptions obtainable by processing information about the content or meaning of books. There is an obvious analogy to human memory: A memory trace containing information about an item's meaning is more likely to be recalled than a memory trace containing only information about physical attributes shared with other items stored in memory.

Later on, I will elaborate on the ease with which we remember extensively processed events. We will encounter this again in Chapter 4, and examine how people retrieve information from memory. At this point, simply note that, if you possess descriptions of two stored items, the one with a more precise description will be easier to find. Just knowing that what you are trying to recall is, say, colored blue, will be enough if the store contains only one blue item. Otherwise, the item as described is not distinctive enough to be located.

PROCESSING AND REMEMBERING: RESEARCH FINDINGS

The experimental finding that people remember better when asked questions demanding a meaningful understanding has been repeated in a number of separate investigations: It is a highly robust effect. The results confirm that mental processing occurring as one perceives is an important influence upon memory. In a number of studies the effect of processing differences on remembering was found to be even larger than the ratio of roughly three to one in the experiment already described. In addition to the one cited above, Craik and Tulving (1975) performed a number of further studies. In most of the studies the experimenters maintained closer control over the way words were presented than they did in the previous experiment. Students indicated their response to the preceding question ("Is it a . . . ?") by pressing one of two keys, marked "Yes" and "No," as quickly as they could. Some experiments ended with a recognition test, but others used tests of recall—the participants writing down all the words they remembered.

In each of eight separate experiments by Craik and Tulving, people remembered word items following questions about meaning more accurately than items following questions about physical form. In those studies using brief (0.2 second) presentation of the words and individual testing, the student participants always remembered at least twice as many of the words accompanied by meaning questions as of the other items. Indeed, in one experiment students recalled over 13 times as many of the words preceded by questions that concerned meanings. Questions concerning phonemic form (such as, "Does the word rhyme with . . . ?")

always produced better remembering than questions concerning letter case (such as, "In capitals?"), but the meaning questions always led to the highest memory scores of all.

When two words were each preceded by meaningful questions, the more complex or difficult question led to better remembering. In one study students had to say if the word would fit into a particular sentence. This could be simple (for example, "The . . . is torn"), of medium complexity ("The ripe . . . tasted delicious"), or complex ("The small lady angrily picked up the red . . ."). The greater the sentence's complexity, the larger the proportion of words recalled. This finding indicates that when each of a number of events is processed on the basis of its meaning, the items most accurately recalled are those most extensively processed.

Processing and Remembering in Children

Children as well as adults can benefit from processing what they see. In one study, 5-year-olds looked at pictures of common objects in pairs (Turnure, Buium, & Thurlowe, 1976). Some children were simply told to verbally label the objects, saying the words the pictures represented. Two other groups of children were told to join together the object words by sentences. For example, when the two pictures in a pair showed a piece of soap and a jacket, the sentence linking them might be "The soap is hiding in the jacket." Children in one of these groups repeated sentences that the experimenter provided; others created their own sentences. Five-year-olds in a fourth group were asked *what* and *why* questions about the relationship between the two objects. For instance, a child might be asked "What is the soap doing under the jacket?" or "Why is the soap in the jacket?"

None of the children knew in advance that memory of the items would be tested, but after all 21 pairs of items were presented, the experimenter showed each child 1 item from every pair and asked the child to recall the object shown with it. The purpose of the study was to discover whether the different mental processing required by the four tasks the children performed while looking at the pictures would affect the number of items recalled.

In fact, there were big differences between the groups. Children who simply gave word labels for the objects recalled only 1 out of the 21 items, on average. Children who repeated sentences provided by the experimenter recalled an average of 3 items. Those who made up their own sentences linking the 2 objects performed much better, recalling 8 items on average. The highest recall levels were achieved by children who answered questions about the 2 objects: They remembered around 16 out of the 21 items. The large differences between the groups emerged despite the fact that all the children saw precisely the same pictures for an equal amount of time. The different amounts of mental processing demanded by the different tasks children performed while inspecting the pictures led to large variations in remembering. Note that the final condition, which involved answering questions, provided a highly effective and practical method for helping 5-year-olds to remember.

An especially effective practical way to help a young child remember is to engage the child in a task with goals genuinely meaningful to him or her. Some youngsters, in a study conducted in the U.S.S.R. (Istomina, 1975, first published in 1948), listened to lists of five words for common objects (such as, carrot, milk, socks). Sixty seconds afterwards the children were asked to say all the words they could remember. Not suprisingly, older children recalled more words than younger children. The oldest subjects, aged between 6 and 7 years, had average recall scores of 2.3 words out of 5. The youngest subjects, who were between 3 and 4 years of age, recalled on the average only 0.6 words. Average recall scores for 4- to 5-year-olds and 5- to 6-year-olds were 1.5 words and 2.0 words out of 5.

Why did the youngest children do so poorly? A possible reason is that this kind of memory task was unfamiliar to them. Alternatively, it is conceivable that the sheer capacity of memory in very young children is simply too small. Some additional findings by Istomina suggest that the first explanation is correct: The strangeness of the test situation was the important factor. Istomina tested children's memories for the same items in a different situation. This time the children were busily engaged in playing a game of shopping. They listened to the same list of words that the other children heard, but instead of having simply to recite the words to the experimenter, they were told to go to the shop and ask for the items on the list.

The two conditions of the study were identical in the timing of the words presented and in the interval between presentation and recall. The difference lay in the meaning and significance of the situation to young children. The second condition, but not the first one, gave them a meaningful goal and a meaningful task to perform.

This had a large effect on children's recall. The average number of words recalled in the second condition was 1.0 (out of 5) for the 3- to 4-year olds, 3.0 for the 4 to 5 group, 3.2 for those 5 to 6, and 3.8 for the 6- to 7-year-olds. Recall scores following both conditions are depicted in Figure 3.1. By inspecting the figures one can compare recall by children of various ages under the different conditions. Although the memory requirements were formally identical, the children's differing perception of the tasks and the consequent differences in processing activities had a large influence on remembering.

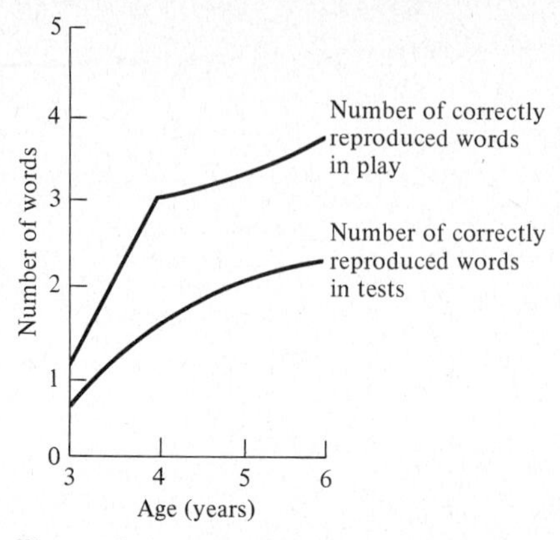

Figure 3.1 Number of words recalled by children in play situation and memory test. *Source:* Istomina (1975).

Remembering Personal Information

Is it easier to remember information that has personal importance? Events having a personal reference to the individual may be especially meaningful and distinctive. Since the self is important in each person's world, items directly referring to one's self "provide a useful device for encoding or interpreting incoming information by virtue of accessing the extensive past experience abstracted in the self. . . ." (Rogers, Kuiper, & Kirker, 1977, p. 679). They asked college students to make one of four kinds of judgments about adjectives displayed. On some occasions the word was preceded by a question about its *physical structure* (type size). The second type of rating task consisted of questions asking whether the adjective *rhymed* with a particular word. A third (semantic) rating task enquired if the word had the same *meaning* as another word. Students in the fourth condition were asked if the adjective described them. Participants responded by pressing a "yes" or "no" button. Afterwards, when the students had rated a total of 40 adjectives, they were asked to write down all the adjectives they could recall, in any order. The students remembered more of the words they rated for similarity of meaning than words rated for physical structure, by a factor of about three to one. An intermediate number of the phonemically rated adjectives were recalled. These findings support the ones obtained by Craik and Tulving (1975) in the similar experiments described earlier in this chapter, but the introduction of the dimension of self-reference led to a further big memory improvement. Compared with the standard semantic (same meaning) condition, subjects recalled nearly twice as many adjectives preceded by a self-reference ("Describes you?") rating task. Clearly, remembering improves considerably when events are not only meaningful but also contain a particular significance in relation to the personal qualities of the individual.

Time as a Possible Factor

Although all the experimental findings described support the view that memory accuracy depends upon the processing activities occurring when an item is perceived, we ought to consider alternative explanations. One possibility might be that memory is related to mental processing not because processing influences remembering directly, but simply because the extensive processing necessary to judge the meaning of something *takes more time* than the perceptual processing required to judge structure. According to this account, the time spent in processing (and attending to) the item, not the processing activities as such, is the key determinant of what will be remembered.

Some data from Craik and Tulving's experiments might appear to support this suggestion. In the studies where words were presented for 0.2 seconds and subjects responded to questions by pressing "Yes" or "No" as quickly as they could, the average time taken to make a response (known as *reaction time*) based on the meaning of a word was greater than the reaction time for deciding a word's phonemic or structural properties. So subjects did spend more time on questions requiring decisions about meaning; the extra time might have been a cause of greater remembering.

Fortunately, Craik and Tulving designed another experiment to decide whether or not the superior recall following meaning questions was primarily due to the greater amount of time involved. Students were asked to make either of two kinds of decisions about words. One task required subjects to judge the meaning of a word (for example, "Does the word fit in the sentence 'The man threw the ball to the . . .'?"). Other questions asked about the structure of the words, and were carefully designed to be more time consuming than the judgments of meaning. The subject was shown a consonant-vowel pattern—for instance CCVVC—before each word. When the word appeared, one had to decide if it fit that pattern (as with BRAIN) or not.

The average reaction time for these questions was about 1.7 seconds, about twice the reaction time for the questions about meaning, which was around 0.8 seconds. If memory following semantic questions is better than memory following structural judgements, an explanation of the previous findings in terms of greater processing time required for semantic judgements would be untenable. In fact, in the present experiment about 75% of the words preceded by meaning questions were recognized, compared with only 50% of the other items. This was despite structural decisions taking twice as long. In short, this result establishes that the better memory for meaningfully processed items is not simply due to greater time.

Intention to Remember

Making a deliberate effort to remember does not always have much effect—a surprising finding! The 5-year-olds who took part in Turnure, Buium, and Thurlow's experiment were *not* told in advance that they would be asked to recall the objects, yet in one condition subjects remembered on average 16 of 21 items. The children in Istomina's studies *did* know that they would be asked to recall the words, but the proportion recalled was very low, especially in the youngest subjects. In some of Craik and Tulving's experiments (although not in others), subjects knew in advance that recall or recognition would be tested. This factor did not have a large impact on the results. Analysis of two of the studies (Experiments 3 and 4) made it possible to compare recall in conditions with and without advance warning of memory tests. Recall was more accurate when subjects had been told in advance, but only by around 10%. Although this is a fairly substantial amount, it is clear that the effects of an intention to remember are relatively small in relation to the much larger effects that we found to be caused by perceptual processing occurring at the input stage. That is not to say that deliberate recall efforts cannot help. However, when an improvement does occur, it may be at least in part because the desire to remember prompts further processing.

Another way to investigate the effects of having an intention to remember is to give subjects financial incentives for accurate recognition. This was done in yet another of Craik and Tulving's (1975) experiments. Students were told they would be rewarded for recognizing words. Rewards of one, three, or six cents were given for each word's recognition. The experiment's design made it possible to compare the effects on word recognition of (a) the type of processing task and (b) the size of the reward. The results were unambiguous. Level of reward did not influence remembering at all, but the effects of the different kinds of processing were comparable to those observed in Craik and Tulving's other studies. In short, the findings provide a further indication that the direct outcome of differences in intent to remember, as manipulated by the incentives, are small or nonexistent.

WHAT INPUT PROCESSING ACHIEVES

Craik and Lockhart (1972) originally claimed that remembering was largely determined by the *depth* of perceptual processing occurring at the input time. This view has encountered various problems, but the basic idea, that remembering depends largely upon the mental processing one undertakes (consciously or otherwise) while perceiving information, is definitely sound.

Memory representations based on limited input processing may be quite adequate when information needs only a few seconds' retention. However, forgetting is usually rapid. For many practical short-term memory requirements, restricted processing may be sufficient. For example, when we look up a telephone number to make a call, we normally retain the number as a list of random digits. When the digit sequence is retained long enough to make the call, it does not matter that rapid forgetting occurs.

If information does not have to be retained for more than a few seconds, it would be wasteful to use up a large proportion of limited processing capacity in order to analyze it. The capacity available for input processing is strictly limited, and it is more economical to restrict our use of that capacity for extensive processing of information that does have to be remembered for longer periods of time. Otherwise, the situation would be a little like that of a librarian who has large piles of books unavailable to borrowers simply because there is not sufficient time for cataloging. If the library receives a larger number of new items each day than there is cataloging capacity available, a bottleneck occurs. In these circumstances the librarian may decide that some of the items in the library (for example, the daily newspapers) need not receive the same cataloging books receive. Thus the limited cataloging capacity is reserved for those items most clearly meriting it. It may be often necessary to be similarly selective with human memory, processing some items at input more fully than others.

TRACE DISTINCTIVENESS

Why does extensive input processing make it more likely that an item will be remembered?

One possible reason is that the more processing taking place, the greater the number of information aspects getting recorded. This increases the number of ways the item in memory can be retrieved or located. We will return to the question of retrieval in Chapter 4, noting here that one effect of exensive coding is to make the memory representation of a retained item more distinctive than it would otherwise be. By distinctive I mean noticeable; easy to discern or find. Something is distinctive if it stands out from other items, perhaps because it is clearly different from them. The description of a retained item in memory will be distinctive if it specifies one particular item and no others. By analogy, if you are looking for a library book and the only description of it you have is a dark blue color, or 250 pages long, you may fail to find the book you seek—simply because there are a number of other items matching the same description. However, if you know the book is about the life of Samuel Johnson, you are much more likely to find it, because the description of the book is more precise. Note that the latter is a *semantic* description: It relates to *meaningful content.* The alternative descriptions refer to physical or structural attributes. Semantic descriptions of items stored in memory are generally more effective than physical descriptions for identifying uniquely the particular item we seek.

Remembering Physical Descriptions

If memory representations of items' structural aspects are fragile and easily disrupted, we might well ask why they are stored at all. Most pertinently, the more descriptions of an item we possess, the better our chances of retrieving the item from memory quickly. If one description of a stored item is not sufficient, another description might be more successful.

Secondly, very often items only need retention for a brief period; in such a case, a brief holding mechanism is quite adequate. A simple means to keep information in memory for a few seconds suffices until capacity for more extensive processing becomes available. If necessary, an item can be rehearsed, maintaining it for a few seconds more. Findings obtained by Kintsch and Bushke (1969) are consistent with this account. If, by the end of this period, there is no need to keep the item in memory, it may safely be forgotten. In brief, then, processing of the physical characteristics, although inadequate for ensuring permanent memory availability, is satisfactory for keeping items a few seconds or so. For long-term remembering, processing that results in meaningful attributes being recorded is more effective.

There is some uncertainty about what actually happens to the memory traces of those items that are available in memory for only a few seconds. It is possible that the memory trace simply decays. Alternatively, the trace may remain but become inaccessible and impossible to locate, rather like the way a particular book in a library containing millions of volumes becomes very hard to find if all we know about it is its blue color. In these circumstances we might say that the book is, to all intents, lost. An analogous situation might exist with memory items no longer remembered.

As I have said, items retained in memory on the basis of meaning descriptions are more distinctive, and hence easier to locate, than items that have undergone more restricted input processing and are described in physical terms. But there are exceptions. A famous one occurs in Proust's describing how the taste and smell of madeleines brought back vivid memories of an earlier time:

> No sooner had the warm liquid, and the crumbs with it, touched my palate than a shudder ran through my whole body, and I stopped, intent upon the extraordinary changes that were taking place. . . .
>
> Undoubtedly, what is thus palpitating in the depths of my being must be the image, the visual memory which, *being linked to that taste*, has tried to follow it into my conscious mind. . . .
>
> And suddenly the memory returns. The taste was that of the little crumb of madeleine which on Sunday mornings at Combray . . . when I went to say good day to her in her bedroom my Aunt Leonie used to give me . . .
>
> And once I had recognized the taste of the crumb of madeleine . . . immediately the old grey house upon the street, where her room was, rose up like the scenery of a theatre. . . .
>
> (Marcel Proust, *Remembrance of Things Past*)

In Proust's description, the taste and smell of the madeleines served as cues for locating large quantities of memory-store material. Perhaps that particular combination of taste and smell was unique, and therefore highly distinctive. Experimental research has confirmed that physical memory traces can be highly distinctive in some cases, making the information represented accessible for long periods of time.

To return once again to the library analogy: Imagine it containing books of several different colors, but only one book colored pink. In that event, a description of that particular book's color is quite sufficient for locating the required item. Indeed, it is reliably observed (and was noted by Helena Von Restorff in 1933) that in any list of similar items, one distinctive from the others will be especially easily remembered. Whenever memory descriptions are based on analyses of distinctive structural characteristics, they are easy to locate within the mass of other items in memory, and may be as easily remembered as items described by their meanings. The greater recall normally following questions requiring meaning analysis is not necessarily due to semantic processing. It may simply be that semantic input processing produces particularly distinctive memory traces. However, as we shall discover in Chapter 5, the distinctiveness of materials in memory is not determined entirely by input processing. It also depends on the kind of search strategy carried out to locate and retrieve items.

Chapter 4 Activities That Aid Memory

INTRODUCTION

What activities do people perform to help themselves remember? The previous chapter demonstrated that memory depends largely upon the way events are processed when first perceived. This chapter describes some of the actions one can do to help effectively process materials. Various activities maximize input processing, and thereby increase recall.

Much of our evidence about processing comes from an unusual and artificial task. Typically, subjects in the experiments I will mention were asked a question about a word, and then shown it briefly. Situations like this are rare in real life: Most of the things we want to remember are not preceded by questions about them! However, input processing can be induced by other, more common, activities. A few of the experiments described in the previous chapter did draw upon realistic everyday activities: for example, Istomina's play situation in which young children were told to go to the store and buy various items. Tasks where brief item presentation is preceded by a question are useful for experimental psychologists wishing to investigate mental processing, but such tasks are rare in everyday life. In the present chapter we shall introduce a wider range of activities and give a more realistic indication of the everyday ways people actually behave to ensure that information and events receive the kinds of processing that lead to accurate remembering.

A number of things people do can influence what they remember. Most of the activities I shall describe are ones performed with a degree of conscious intent. However, some of the activities may occur automatically, and they do not always require conscious awareness.

The term *activity* has a range of meanings. In the present chapter it refers to behaviors related to cognition—rehearsing, labeling and organizing materials, and finding connections mediating between items, for instance. Although imprecise, activity is a more direct description of what a person performs than the term *processing*, because mental processing as such is not actually observable, but merely inferred. When an activity is fairly complex and involves a number of elements, it is customary to say that the individual is following a strategy or plan. Again, a plan can be called a mnemonic technique or method if it is known to aid memory.

Various activities are known to affect memory. The value of a particular activity depends upon a number of factors. In the following pages we will encounter some evidence demonstrating that what an individual recalls is influenced by various personal attributes. For instance, knowledge related to the newly perceived information is particularly important. As a general rule, a particular plan or strategy will aid remembering if it leads to processing that results in distinctive and retrievable descriptions. As we discovered in the previous chapter, semantic (meaningful) descriptions of events tend to be more precise and more specific, and hence more readily located in memory than nonsemantic descriptions.

REHEARSAL

Rehearsal is possibly the most widely used of all the practical activities aiding memory. Research findings confirm that rehearsal is beneficial, and draw attention to considerable variation in different rehearsal activities' effectiveness.

Research involving young children (who do not spontaneously rehearse in the kinds of memory tasks psychologists ask them to perform) has been especially helpful in demonstrating the general effectiveness of rehearsal. For instance, in one study (Keeney, Cannizzo, & Flavell, 1967) it was found that 6- and 7-year-old children, who did *not* rehearse spontaneously, recalled all the simple memory test items in less than 40% of the trials. Children of the same age who *did* rehearse were correct in 60%. The children who did not rehearse were then trained to do so. Subsequently, they too recalled all items correctly in over 60% of the trials.

Mentally retarded people, also, can gain from being shown how to rehearse. Lengthy training is not necessary, and simple instructions to whisper the names of items are often effective. Rehearsal can be useful for helping people learn and retain various kinds of materials, including highly meaningful information. In a study that was published in 1917, A. I. Gates found that children and adolescents learned prose passages most easily if they spent as much as 60% of the time reciting the material aloud, rather than passively reading.

Why does rehearsal help people remember? It is useful to distintuish between two functions of rehearsal. One, called *maintenance rehearsal* by some writers, simply keeps repeating the items, increasing the amount of time they are available. According to Baddeley (1976), the memory system has a mechanism which he calls a *rehearsal buffer* to permit this kind of rehearsal. A second possible function of rehearsal is to contribute to item processing. This occurs, for example, when rehearsal involves some form of grouping, organization, or elaboration of the materials, requiring further processing. When items are rehearsed in groups, the meanings, connections, and relationships between materials are especially likely to become apparent, and the accompanying processing may yield distinctive item descriptions one may readily locate in memory.

There has been some controversy over whether rehearsal leads to improved remembering only if it involves extended processing (*elaboration*) of the items, or whether maintenance rehearsal *alone* can improve remembering. Craik and Watkins (1973), who claimed that the effects of maintenance rehearsals are strictly limited, found that simply repeating word items did not affect the probability of recall. However, in another study, Nelson (1977) obtained results he interpreted as demonstrating that repetition can produce better remembering even when it does *not* involve the materials receiving further processing.

It is not easy to decide which competing claim is correct. It is difficult to design tasks where repetition occurs but is definitely not accompanied by extended processing. In the task performed in Nelson's study, the period of time between each successive word item was 5 seconds. Although the task instructions did not demand further processing, the participants did have some time available to think about the words.

Rehearsal and Consolidation

Rehearsal provides a possible explanation for some items presented in a memory experiment being better remembered than others—a frequent result. Consider, for instance, the finding by Howe (1965), described in Chapter 2 (p. 14). Immediately after a list was presented, students' memory for the early items was firmer, or more consolidated, than memory of consonants occurring in a later part of the same list. If only some of the consonants had to be recalled as soon as presentation of the list was completed, the later (most recent) list items were more accurately remembered than the early ones, possibly because the interval of time between presentation and recall of the late items was smaller. But the late consonants were much more readily forgotten than the early ones. Telling a subject to recall other letters first had a much more damaging effect upon memory for the late than for the early items.

The effect can be seen in Figure 4.1. The slopes of the lines representing early (*P*1) and late (*P*3) items are clearly different, and a crossover occurs.

Differences in rehearsal provide a possible explanation of the greater degree of consolidation in memory between the items at the beginning of a list (*P*1) and the late items in a list (*P*3) in Figure 4.1. In the experiment, one consonant was presented per second, a rate which allowed subjects some time for rehearsing. A common strategy is to rehearse letters in groups, starting with the first item. For example, with

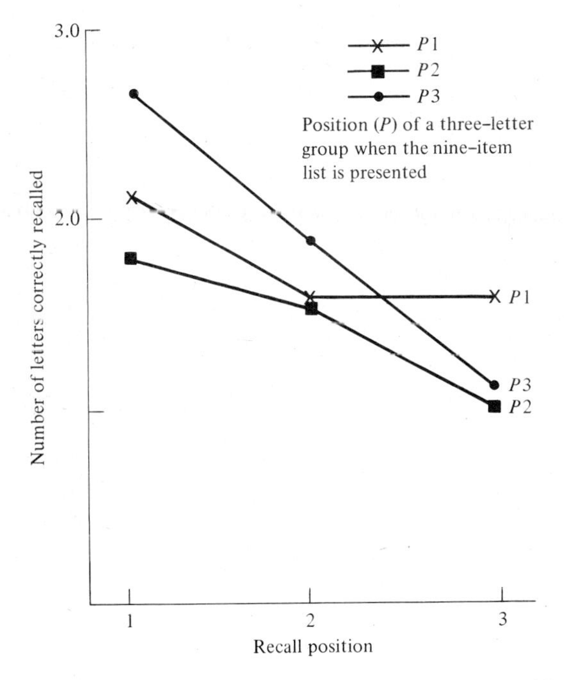

Figure 4.1 Recall as a function of recall position and position of presentation. *Source:* Howe (1965).

the list B X A G C D L M, actual rehearsals during the presentation period might be something like this:

B BX BXA BXAG

A rehearsal strategy like this one favors the early items; items toward the end of a list receive fewer rehearsals. Hence the suggestion that differences in rehearsal are caused by more consolidation of early items in a list, making them less vulnerable to forgetting than the late items.

A further experiment by Howe (1967a) examined the suggestion that rehearsal of the early items was the cause of their becoming more consolidated in memory. If the greater consolidation of some items is caused by their receiving more rehearsal than others, we would expect differences to disappear if every item is rehearsed identically. This is just what was observed in the experiment. In one of the two conditions, subjects chose their own rehearsal strategy. As in the earlier study, early list items became more consolidated than later ones. However, in the other condition, participants were told to rehearse each item aloud as soon as it appeared, and only that item. This procedure ensured that all were equally rehearsed. In these circumstances the difference between early and late list in degree of consolidation completely disappeared. This finding firmly supports the suggestion that rehearsal is the cause of differences in memory consolidation within short lists.

Differences in the extent of items' rehearsal partly explain the shape of *serial position* curves such as the ones in Figure 2.2 (page 14) in which a list's early and late items are more accurately remembered than middle items. The relatively accurate recall of the early list items (*primacy effect*) may be due to their receiving the greatest amount of rehearsal. The good performance on the most recent items (*recency effect*) can be explained by the relatively short time those items are remembered.

Evidence supporting the suggestion that primary effects seen in serial position curves are caused by rehearsal of the early items was obtained in a study by Rundus (1971). He asked the subjects to rehearse the word items aloud, so the number of rehearsals could be counted. The findings, depicted in Figure 4.2, clearly demonstrate that the separate measures of recall accuracy and number of rehearsals are closely parallel in early items, providing a further indication of a cause-and-effect connection.

The above explanation of the recency effect can be easily tested by delaying recall of late items. The outcome should be to flatten that part of the serial position curve that shows recall of the most recent items. The actual effect can be seen by comparing recall of the late items (*P*3) in Figure 4.1 (p. 41) when they were the final ones to be recalled (*R*3), to recall of the identical items when they were the first to be recalled (*R*1).

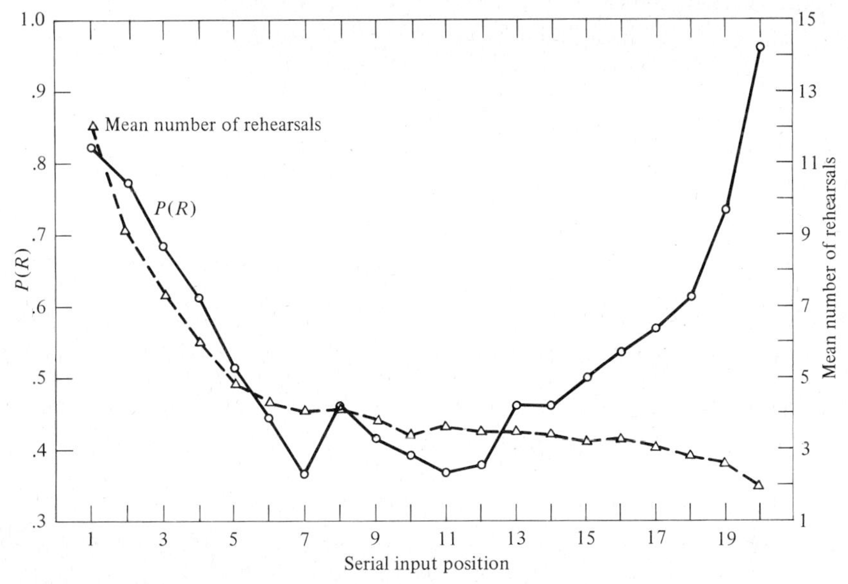

Figure 4.2 Relationship between probability of recall—*P* (*R*)—and number of rehearsals. *Source:* Rundus (1971).

A more direct test of the effect of delayed final items' recall on the recency part of the serial position curve is depicted in Figure 4.3. This illustrates the findings of an experiment by Glanzer and Cunitz (1966). Figure 4.3 shows a delay between presentation of the final items in a list and the instruction to begin recalling simply erased the recency effect.

ORGANIZATION

When entering the library to find a psychology book you are sure to notice that books on psychology are located in a particular part of the library. If you wanted poetry you would look elsewhere. One result of cataloging the books is to make possible their convenient arrangement and organization, facilitating one's finding what one wants.

Stored information processed at input to memory on the basis of meaningful attributes is also organized. This is illustrated in the following passage by J. D. Bransford (1979).

> Imagine that you are asked to perform the following task as quickly as possible: Name a past president of the United States whose name begins with L. Most people are able to answer, "Lincoln." What did you have to do to perform this task? While thinking about this question, try a few more examples: Name a piece of furniture that begins with a C; name a make of car that begins with F; name a piece of clothing that begins with S. (Bransford, 1979, p. 169)

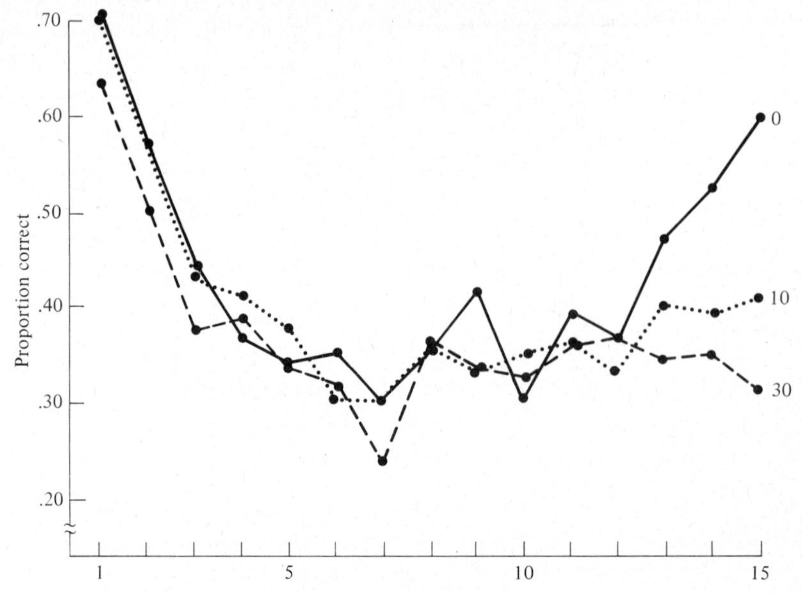

Figure 4.3 Serial position curves, showing effects of 0-, 10-, and 30-second delay between presentation and recall. *Source:* Glanzer and Cunitz (1966).

Bransford's point is that when one is asked questions like these, one does not search through one's entire knowledge before arriving at the correct answer. One need not do so because the knowledge is *organized.* Consequently, when you are asked a question about a U.S. president, you can selectively direct a search for the answer and gain access to knowledge concerning presidents of the U.S. Knowledge can be grouped, ordered, divided, classified, and categorized in various ways, making it easy to retrieve. In consequence, if someone tells me that what I'm trying to remember is a large animal beginning with the letter "T," he may help me to recall the correct item ("Tiger").

Organization and input processing are closely intertwined. In practice, engaging in organizational activities such as grouping, classifying, and categorizing information is a particularly effective kind of behavior for directing input processing. Requiring a student to organize new materials provides a way to ensure they are appropriately analyzed. As a result, each variety of organizational activities can help recall.

Organization helping memory has been amply documented, but it is not always easy to say *how* a particular organizational activity contributes to memory. The precise effects of the various activities differ, although most kinds of organization involve items being processed according to their meaningful qualities. This can make items in memory easier to locate. In some cases, having to categorize items may draw attention to a relationship between them or a shared attribute. Consequently, the information is processed at a more abstract level of analysis.

In other instances, once one becomes aware of a connection between two items, it may be possible to remember them as a single unit. This has obvious advantages. To illustrate this effect, S. Smith (Miller, 1956) trained himself and a number of students to recode sequences of the binary digits 0 and 1. Having established that the memory span for random orderings of sequences of 0s and 1s was around 8 or 9 items, he proceeded to train the students to group the items in pairs and then recode them. Thus 00 was denoted as 0, 01 as 1, 10 as 2, and 11 as 3. In this way an 18-digit sequence, 101000100111001110, reduces to a 9-item list, 220213032. The latter is much easier to remember! Most people find it impossible to remember the complete 18-item list sequence after just one presentation. However, on presentation the sequence can immediately be encoded as a 9-item list, and remembered in that form.

When recall is necessary, the list can be decoded back into the original format. The method may appear clumsy, but if training and practice in encoding is given, it is not difficult. Smith trained both himself and his subjects and, as a result, recall scores greatly increased. If sufficient practice is allowed, it is possible not only to encode pairs of digits as single items, but to recode groups of three, four, or even five digits as one item. By doing so, Smith was able to increase his own memory span for sequences containing the digits 0 and 1 to as many as 40 items. Of course, he did not have to remember 40 separate digits: By recoding each group of 5 digits to a single unit, the number to be stored was reduced to 8.

Activities having the effect of recoding information are not uncommon in everyday life. In Smith's experiment, the outcome of coding was to reduce the number of separate units to be remembered. This was achieved by increasing the size of the units. Similarly, a person can often combine a number of separate items and form a single group. This process is known as *chunking*. A chunk is defined as a body of information which functions as a single group, and can be regarded as forming single items (Miller, 1956). Since a person's memory span (the number of separate items retained in active memory) is strictly limited, chunking, which increases the amount of information in each item and correspondingly decreases the number of separate items, is a particularly valuable way to help a person to remember more.

In practice, the size of chunks is usually decided by processes happening with little or no conscious intention. For example, the sequence T A R G E T can be perceived either as one single word (by people who can read) or as six separate letters (by a child who cannot read but can identify single letters). A child who is learning to read will greatly increase his capacity to remember letter sequences like this one as he learns to identify the words they form.

Psychologists have a sizeable body of knowledge about the effects of organization upon memory. They find people are good at recalling lists of items meaningfully related to one another, even when they cannot make a single unit. For example, words that can be placed into categories are more accurately remembered than lists comprised of unrelated words. When a word sequence has items from a number of different categories, but randomly ordered, the order in which people actually recall the different words indicates that a degree of grouping into categories has taken place: The recall sequences contain word clusters in a single group, showing the person has used his knowledge of the categories as a way to organize the words (Bousfield, 1953). A similar effect is observed when words do not fall into definite categories but are simply related to each other—for example, *table, food* (Jenkins & Russell, 1952). The greater the degree of relationship between pairs of items from a list, the greater the number of words recalled, even when the words are presented not as pairs but in random order (Jenkins, Mink, & Russell, 1958). When words do fall into definite groups, there is more recall clustering, and more items are remembered if the words frequently occur as a response to the category heading (Bousfield, Cohen, & Whitmarsh, 1958). In the category *food,* for example, *bread* is a more frequent response than *avocado.* Lists containing items sharing a common category (for example, *bed* and *chair,* both subsumed within *furniture*) are more accurately recalled than lists of words related to each other but not sharing membership in a single category (say, *bed* and *dream*) (Cofer, 1965).

Subjective Organization

In everyday situations, people often find ways to organize materials they wish to learn even when the items do not fall into clear categories and there is no obvious organization. This tendency for individuals to impose their own organization upon things they need to remember was demonstrated in a study by Endel Tulving (1962). The experimenter presented a list containing 16 words, chosen at random, and afterwards each subject attempted to recall them. Then the words were presented again, but in a completely different order. Once more, the subjects tried to recall them and there was a further presentation of the words, yet again in a different order. This procedure continued for a total of 16 trials.

As you would expect, the accuracy of recall improved from trial to trial. However, Tulving did not simply measure the number of items recalled. He was much more interested in the *order* in which words were remembered. He found that, although the order of presentation changed entirely from one trial to the next, the order in which people actually recalled the words in successive trials showed considerable constancy. Pairs of words together in the recall sequence following one presentation tended to be recalled together on the next trial. Over successive trials, participants had a strong tendency to recall the items in the same order.

Tulving noted that his findings indicated individual subjects must have been relating the words to each other or connecting them, and thus processing a number of words together as something approaching a single unit or chunk. He stated that people impose *subjective organization* on materials in tasks of this kind. He also noticed that as recall increased from one trial to the next, so did the amount of subjective organization. Moreover, those people displaying high degrees of subjective organization were better at recalling the words than other participants.

The findings of Tulving's study show that remembering is related to the organization people impose upon materials they learn: It seems likely that subjective organization causes increased recall. We cannot be certain of this, however, because there might be an alternative reason for the observed relationship between organization and recall. For instance, it is conceivable that improved recall is simply caused by the repeated presentation of the items, which also leads to increases in subjective organization. We need a way to check the plausibility of this suggestion.

To assess this possibility, Tulving designed a study in which repetition of the materials was *not* accompanied by consistently increasing organization. In this study (Tulving, 1966) there were 12 presentations of an 18-word list. Each presentation was followed by an attempt at recall. Some of the participants had been exposed to the words on 6 previous trials, and they thus saw these words half again as many times as did the other subjects (18 presentations compared with 12). If repetition is the main cause of improved recall, we would expect those participants who inspected the words on 18 occasions to do considerably better than those only receiving 12 presentations.

However, those people who saw the words on all 18 occasions saw them occurring in pairs consisting of a word together with a single letter on the first six of the trials. During these trials the word-letter pairs had to be pronounced aloud by each participant. It was thus impossible for subjects to organize the word items at this stage in a way compatible with the organization in the second part of the task. Therefore, if increased organization, rather than repeated presentation, explained the memory improvements during the earlier experiment, subjects who received all 18 presentations would not recall appreciably more words than those looking at the items only 12 times.

In fact, this is precisely what Tulving found. The two groups of participants did not differ in the number of words they recalled, despite the fact that one group saw the words 50% more.

This finding, depicted in Figure 4.4, clearly supports the view that learners' increases in the organization of materials, and not simple repetition, account for steady improvement in recall.

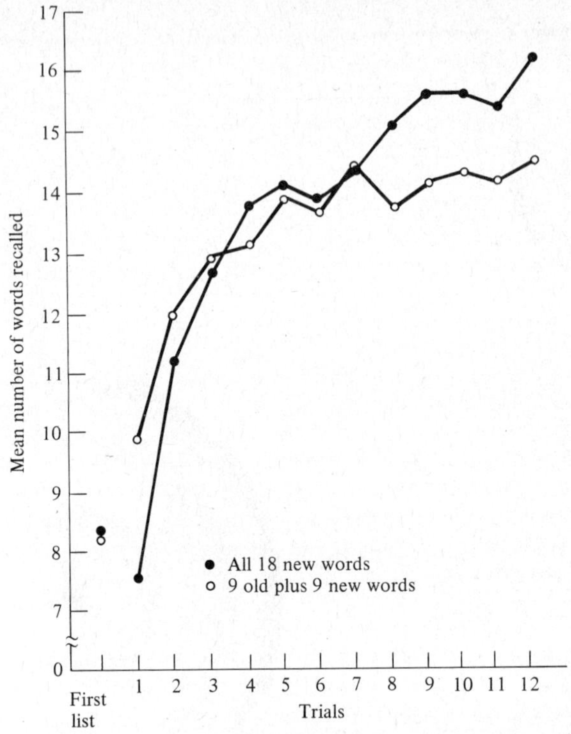

Figure 4.4 Rate of learning for 18-word lists. *Source:* Tulving (1966).

Further research indicates, however, that matters are not quite so straightforward as this suggests. For example, during Tulving's 1966 experiment the changes between the first 6 and the subsequent 12 trials not only prevented subjective organization, but may have also confused the participants. People are quite likely to become confused when a new list of words contains some but not all of the same items as the previous list (Roberts, 1969; Slamecka, Moore, & Carey, 1972). When people doing similar tasks are carefully told in advance how the second stage differs from the early part, recall tends to improve (Wood & Clark, 1969; Novinsky, 1972). However, although the later findings suggest that repetition as such is more effective than Tulving's results suggested, his conclusion that a person's subjective organization makes a contribution to learning does remain true.

Other Questions About Organization

Remembering can be increased either by organizing activities undertaken by the individual learner, as in Tulving's experiments, or by organization evident in the way materials are presented. We might expect the organizational activities a person undertakes for herself to be more effective than organizational schemes imposed upon her, and the findings of an experiment by Mandler and Pearlstone (1966) indicate that this is so. Subjects were given packs of 52 cards; on each, there appeared a single noun. Half of the participants were told to sort the cards into groups or categories, between 2 and 7 in number, on any basis they liked. To test how well the categorized words were remembered, each person was given exactly the same words again but in a completely different random order. The instruction was to group the cards once more, using precisely the same categories developed previously. This procedure was repeated until the participant succeeded in categorizing all 52 nouns identically on 2 successive occasions.

The other group of subjects received the same 52 cards, but instead of being in random order the words were already divided into categories (by one of the participants in the other group). The memory task for the second group of subjects was, like that of the others, to achieve 2 identical categorizations of the words on successive presentations. However, unlike the other subjects, participants in the second group started with a grouping devised by another person.

There was a large recall difference between the groups. People who organized the words themselves achieved the criterion of two identical orderings in just half as many trials as the other subjects. Clearly, organizing materials for oneself was much more effective than following someone else's organizational scheme.

If you are organizing materials, is there an optimum number of categories? Research by G. Mandler (1968) shows that, concerning lists of around 50 words, the more categories the better—up to about 7 categories. There was then a high positive correlation between recall accuracy and the number of categories people used. When unlimited categories were allowed, more than 7 did not produce further memory improvements. Notice that this number—around 7—is broadly similar to the memory span: the greatest number of single units remembered without error when information is presented and remembered over a short period of time.

It might be possible to improve memory still further, Mandler suggested, if items are not simply divided into categories but organized hierarchically, at more than one level. For instance, 100 words might be divided into 5 groups, with 20 items in each. Each group could be further divided into 5 subcategories, each containing 4 items. Does hierarchical, multilevel organization of this kind produce further improvements in remembering? To answer this question, Gordon Bower and others (Bower, Clark, Lesgold, & Winzenz, 1969) devised a number of *conceptual hierarchies* for word items. The hierarchy shown in Figure 4.5 illustrates how the words were organized.

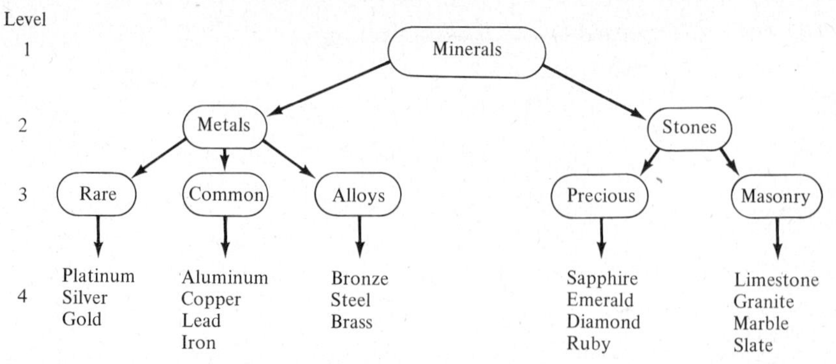

Figure 4.5 Hierarchical organization of mineral words. *Source:* Bower, Clark, Lesgold, and Winzenz (1969).

The items in this particular word hierarchy are all minerals: however, some of them are metals and others are stones. The metals are further divided into rare, common, and alloys. The stones are all either precious or masonry.

Hierarchical organization's effectiveness was tested in a number of experiments. Bower and his colleagues found that presenting materials in this manner did lead to considerably higher levels of recall than alternative arrangements. For instance, in one experiment, people recalled an average of only 21 out of 112 words when words were randomly arranged. They recalled 73 words from hierarchical presentations. After two presentations most subjects who saw the words organized in a hierarchical arrangement such as the one shown in Figure 4.5 recalled all 112 of the words. Those given randomly arranged items recalled only around 40% of the identical words at this stage, although both groups of subjects had the same amount of time to study the materials.

ORGANIZATION AND MEDIATION IN LANGUAGE STRUCTURE

Presentation within the framework of structured language is a particularly effective way to organize information. Each of us knows a great deal about language structure: Our knowledge of formal grammar may be very limited, but we find it easy to spot a word sequence not obeying the rules of structured language. If the information we want to remember is provided in a form that does follow the familiar structure of our own language, perhaps our knowledge of the language will help to organize the materials, and make them easier to remember.

Effects of Organization in Language: Approximations to English

The findings of an experiment reported in 1950 by Miller and Selfridge confirm that word sequences following the rules of language are considerably better remembered than random sequences of the same words. A number of word sequences, known as *approximations to English,* were made by asking people to combine words in ways that followed some of the constraints of the English language. For example, in order to construct a third-order approximation-to-English sequence, one would be given two words (for example, *family was*) and asked to supply a following word that would form a grammatical sentence. If one contributed, say, *large,* the next participant would be shown the two-word sequence *was large,* and asked to supply the next item. After a number of people had contributed words, a third-order sequence would have been made, such as the following one:

> family was large dark animal come roaring down
> the middle of my friends love books passionately
> every kiss is fine

As you can see, the sequence is similar to English: Its structure does approximate that of the language. The higher the order of approximation, the closer a sequence follows the form of grammatical English. To make a list of *n*th order of approximation, people would be asked to contribute single words to sequences of *n-1* grammatically structured words. Figure 4.6 shows how word sequence recall of varying lengths was influenced by order of approximation. The higher the order of approximation, the larger the number of words one remembers.

Grammatical Structure

Presenting information in language form may aid recall not only because the structure is increased, but because the materials are more meaningful. In most circumstances it is impossible to disentangle these aspects of language, but the findings of an interesting experiment by Marks and Miller (1964) demonstrated that grammatical but not meaningful sentences, such as:

> Noisy flushes emit careful floods
> Trains steal elephants around the highways

are more accurately recalled than sequences comprised of the same words in random order, for example:

> Between gadgets highway passengers the steal
> Neighbors sleeping noisy wake parties

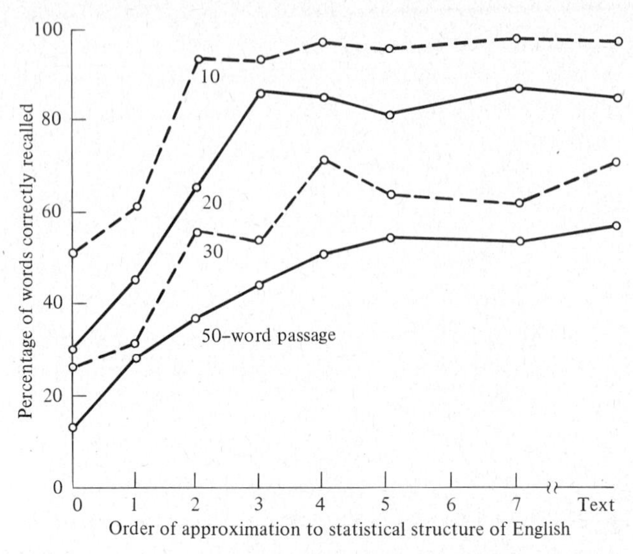

Figure 4.6 Word recall from lists at different orders of approximation to English. *Source:* Miller and Selfridge (1950).

However, sentences that are both grammatical and meaningful are most accurately recalled. Examples are:

> Noisy parties wake sleeping neighbors
> Accidents kill motorists on the highways

Even nonword syllables are more accurately recalled when they are presented within a kind of grammatical structure (Epstein, 1961), such as:

> The Yigs wur vulmy rixing hum.

A Narrative Strategy

A striking demonstration of the outcome of the meaningful processing and organization imposed by language structure was found in a study by Bower and Clark (1969). College students followed a strategy involving making narratives to join words. All participants learned 12 lists, containing 10 concrete nouns. Half the students were told to make up a narrative story connecting the 10 words in each list. For example, from a list composed of the words *vegetable, instrument, college, carrot, nail, basin, merchant, queen, scale, goat,* one student produced the following narrative:

A *vegetable* can be a useful *instrument* for a *college* student. A *carrot* can be a *nail* for your fence or *basin.* But a *merchant* of the *Queen* would *scale* the fence and feed the carrot to a *goat.*

After a couple of practice trials, students found it fairly easy to make their own narratives, and it took them around a minute and a half. For each list, every subject made a new narrative story, starting with the first word and including the other items in the order in which they appeared. After a student had completed the narrative for each of the 12 lists, he was asked to recall the words. At this stage, students recalled over 90% of the items, on average.

Each of the other students, who formed a control group, was "yoked" to a subject in the first (experimental) group: They were allowed the same amount of time to study each list as the students making narratives. However, students in the control group received no instructions to form narratives or to adopt any other strategy. Following the presentation of each list, the control group subjects were tested for recall and, like the narrative-makers, recalled around 90% of the words correctly.

After all 12 word lists had been presented and recalled, the students in both groups tried to write down as many as they could of all 120 words in the 12 lists. Despite the fact that the two groups had not differed in recall accuracy when tested immediately after each list, there was a vast difference between the narrative-making students and the other subjects at this later stage. This can be seen in Figure 4.7. The narrative group recalled from two to four times as many words as the other participants, although the study time was identical in the two groups.

The difference in eventual recall, favoring students following narrative strategy, is robust as well as large. On a number of occasions I have repeated the experiment with undergraduate practical classes. Each time, in the final test, the narrative-makers have recalled at least twice as many words as the other participants.

Notice that the value of this highly effective student strategy is not apparent immediately; that is clear from the similar achievement on the immediate recall test following each separate list by the two student groups. It is not until later that the great advantage of the narrative strategy becomes obvious. This is equally true of many good strategies.

For this reason, immature learners, or people who only test themselves immediately after studying the materials they want to remember, may never become aware of just how effective certain learner strategies can be in the long run.

Mediating Functions of Language

Why is the narrative strategy such an effective one? One reason is that it provides help by using the organizational structure of language. At the same time, learners have to look for ways to join the words to each other, and attend to their meaningful attributes. Both the connecting and language organization functions are also present in a similar, but simpler,

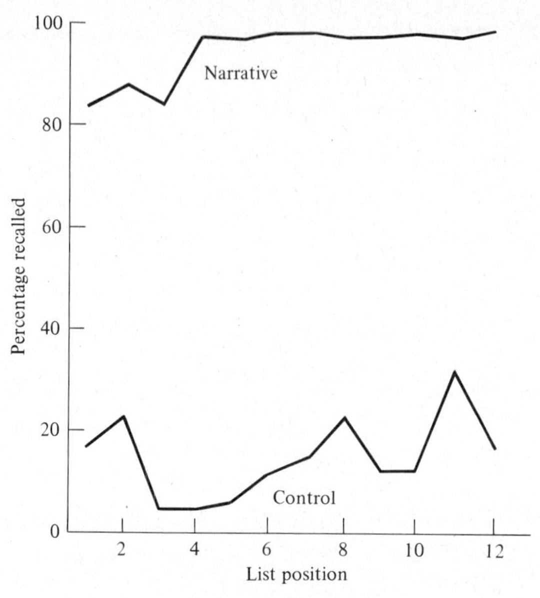

Figure 4.7 Words recalled following narrative and control conditions.
Source: Bower and Clark (1969).

strategy that Jensen and Rohwer (1963, 1965) found to be highly effective for helping young learners and mentally retarded adults.

Mentally retarded people performed a simple learning task, trying to remember lists made up of eight pairs of words. Some of the subjects were given no instructions about how to learn; other participants were provided with sentences that served to mediate between or join together the two words in each pair. For example, for the word pair *donkey-chair* the sentence "The *donkey* kicked the *chair*" fulfills the mediating function. The experimenters found providing participants with mediating sentences improved learning considerably. Subjects who were given sentences required only half the time taken by the others to learn the complete list, and they made only about one-fifth the number of errors.

In many everyday situations, intelligent adult learners engage in activities and strategies leading to meaningful processing without explicit instructions to do so. When adults learn lists of word pairs like the ones presented by Jensen and Rohwer, they may spontaneously form linking sentences or adopt an equally effective alternative strategy; for example, searching for connections between items, or forming visual images. Nevertheless, in the absence of explicit instructions to follow a strategy, even the most intelligent adults do not always use the most effective strategy, as the results of the study by Bower and Clark clearly demonstrate.

CONCLUSION

In general, the activities and strategies most likely to be successful in a particular situation are those most effective in leading to the appropriate processing of materials to be remembered. The value of a particular strategy depends on, among other things, its suitability to the age and abilities of the user. Jensen and Rohwer found their sentence-linking strategy was highly successful in 11-year-old children, but ineffective for 17-year-olds (perhaps because, in the absence of supplied sentences, they formed their own equally effective strategies) and also ineffective for very young children, aged around 4 years (who were too young to fully understand the procedure).

Sentences were also found to be relatively ineffective for young children in the study by Turnure, Buium, and Thurlowe (1976) described in Chapter 3 (p. 30). In that study, 5-year-olds who either generated their own sentences or used sentences the experimenter supplied for them recalled about twice as many items as children who simply named the items (pictures of common objects) they were shown. However, the sentence conditions were far less effective than the one where children tried to answer questions concerning the relationship between two items (for example, "What is the soap doing under the jacket?"). Probably, questions like these were especially effective for 5-year-olds, because they succeeded in getting the children to process the items in a way highly meaningful to them.

We mentioned in Chapter 3 that having an intention to remember does not, in itself, greatly affect recall. What is more important is the kind of processing activity undertaken. The research described in the present chapter amply demonstrates that information processed in a way leading to retention in a distinctive and readily retrievable form is more likely to be remembered.

We have not yet mentioned one important group of activities strongly affecting memory. These involve using visual imagery, a topic we turn to in Chapter 5.

Chapter 5
The Functions of Imagery

SOME MNEMONIC TECHNIQUES

In Chapter 1 I described a mnemonic device for improving memory, called the place method or method of loci. A person using this technique forms visual images of the objects to be remembered. In one investigation of the place method's effectiveness (Ross & Lawrence, 1968), students were told to imagine 40 familiar locations around their university campus. Then a list of 40 objects was presented, at a rate of 12 items per minute. When the students tried to recall the objects immediately afterwards, they remembered 38 out of 40, on average. Even after a day's delay, average recall was 36 items, a much higher level of performance than is usually found.

There are a number of mnemonic techniques following a visual image strategy. Some of the techniques are described in this chapter.

Strategies using visual imagery have some elements in common with the rehearsing, mediating, and other organizing activities described in the previous chapter. Imagery strategies, like the others, require attending to items and engaging in activities involving mental processing.

As a result, memory traces are formed describing important aspects or attributes of the materials to be remembered. A visual image evokes the *appearance* of concrete objects. Like those strategies depending upon analysis of the word items' meanings, imagery strategies involve levels of processing that extensively analyze attributes.

The Rhyme Method

Describing an actual mnemonic technique will clarify matters. One imagery mnemonic, known for reasons which will become obvious as the rhyme method, can be used to learn ordered word sequences. An everyday application might be remembering the items in a shopping list. To use the rhyme method, you start by learning a very simple rhyme, as follows:

One is a bun
Two is a shoe
Three is a tree
Four is a door
Five is a hive
Six are sticks
Seven is heaven
Eight is a gate
Nine is wine
Ten is a hen

Once the rhyme has been learned and practiced so each word is readily evoked by the corresponding number (and vice versa) with little effort, it can be used to aid remembering. The next step is to form a strong visual image for each of the nouns in the rhyme. Images should be of particular objects, and should be as clear and striking as possible. For example:

> Think, for example, not of "*bun*" in general, but of a very particular bun. Visualize the bun if you can. Is it large or small? Brown or yellow? Has it raisins? Has it icing? One is a bun." (Hunter, 1964, p. 288)

People differ in their ease in forming visual images, but given sufficient time and practice, most people can make images of concrete objects without difficulty. Now imagine that you must remember to buy the following items, and that their order corresponds to the sequence of shops to be visited and the positions of different kinds of merchandise in the shops.

1. Sugar
2. Bread
3. Eggs

4. Bananas
5. Pen
6. Envelopes
7. Toothbrush
8. Soap
9. Sandpaper
10. Paint

To learn the list, all that you have to do is to take one item at a time and form a clear visual image of the pair containing the appropriate list object and the corresponding item in the rhyme, for instance:

Bun - Sugar
Shoe - Bread
Tree - Eggs, and so on

Thus for sugar you make a visual image of sugar in connection with the unique, striking bun you have already imaged. Your combined image might contain your bun covered with a vast pile of sugar. You next create an image combining the second list item, bread, and shoe (corresponding with the second list item), and proceed in this manner, making images for each of the succeeding pairs.

Providing sufficient time is allowed for image making (around five seconds per pair, or longer), this method is highly effective. When you want to remember a particular item, say the third one, you simply identify the image for the corresponding rhyme item (*tree*), and inspection reveals the linked image of the tree and the eggs, showing you the third item in the shopping list is *eggs*. On several occasions, as a class demonstration, I have compared the rhyme method with a rote learning condition in which students simply inspect and rehearse the items. The rhyme method has always produced considerably more accurate recall.

The advantage of the rhyme mnemonic over learning by rote is largest if there is an interval of time between learning and recall. Imagery techniques, like the narrative method and other strategies described in the previous chapter, display their greatest superiority after information is remembered over a fairly long period.

Figure 5.1 shows the findings of a study comparing learning under imagery and control conditions (Bugelski, Kidd, & Segmen, 1968). Notice that imagery instructions led to markedly improved recall when the items were presented at a rate of one every eight seconds. It is difficult to form images during a fast presentation. In the fastest condition (an item every two seconds), there may be insufficient time to form clear visual images.

Why is the rhyme method effective? There are a number of probable factors. Having formed an image of, say, a tree and eggs in combina-

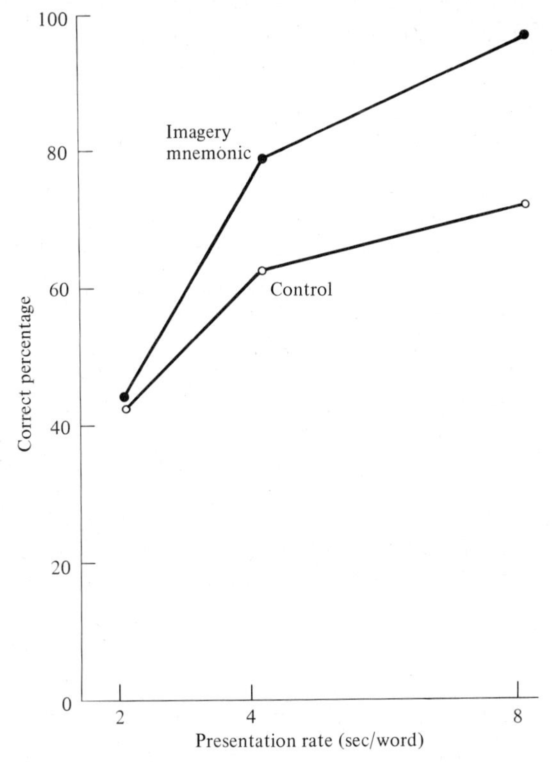

Figure 5.1 Words recalled following imagery and control conditions.
Source: Bugelski, Kidd, and Segmen (1968).

tion, inspection of the image leads easily to object identification. The linked image's availability reduces the difficulty of locating the correct item. In other words, the image serves as a route to the stored representation of the item required. It is necessary to find the linked image corresponding to each number, but this step has already been well learned, with the help of the rhyme. Once the first link between a number and the corresponding image has been learned, it can be used again and again with different lists. In fact, the rhyme method may be used to learn a whole series of lists, without the error and confusion occurring with rote learning methods. There is no interference between items in successive lists.

The Link Method

One problem with the rhyme method is that a certain amount of time is necessary for learning the "one is a bun" rhyme at the outset. An alternative method using linked images for learning ordered lists requires no advance preparation at all. It is called the *link method,* and it is extremely simple. Assume that you wish to remember the following objects, in order.

bottle
envelope
table
window
book
shirt
watch
truck
leopard
bicycle

With the link method, it is simply necessary to form images of the successive pairs of objects. You can try this right now. It will only take a few minutes! Start by making a visual image of the first pair. In *How to Develop a Super-Power Memory,* author Harry Lorayne (1958), a professional memorist who makes regular stage performances demonstrating striking feats of memory, shows his readers how to begin learning a list containing these items:

> carpet, paper, bottle, bed, fish, chair, window, telephone, cigarette, nail, typewriter, shoe, microphone, pen, television set, plate, doughnut, car, coffee pot, and brick.
>
> The first thing you have to do is to get a picture of the first item, "carpet," in your mind. You all know what a carpet is—so just "see" it in your mind's eye. Don't just see the word "carpet" but actually, for a second, see either any carpet, or a carpet that is in your own home and is therefore familiar to you. . . . You must now *associate* or *link* carpet to, or with, paper. The association must be as *ridiculous as possible.* For example, you might picture the carpet in your home made out of paper. See yourself walking on it, and actually hearing the paper crinkle underfoot. . . . You must actually see this ridiculous picture in your mind for a fraction of a second. . . . As soon as you can see it, stop thinking about it and go on to your next step. (Lorayne, 1958, p. 33)

The next step is to make a link between paper and the next item, bottle. Lorayne suggests making an image of yourself reading a gigantic bottle, in place of paper, or a bottle pouring paper out of its mouth, or a bottle made out of paper. (Lorayne repeatedly stresses the necessity of actually seeing the picture in the mind's eye.) For the next item, bed, a link with bottle might be formed by visualizing sleeping in a large bottle instead of a bed. For the next link, between bed and fish, an image could be formed of a giant fish sleeping in a bed.

Proceed in this manner until you come to the end of the list. Then you can test yourself to see if you can remember all the items.

Most people find this method works extremely well. A small proportion of individuals find it very difficult, if not impossible, to make visual images. However, for the vast majority of people the link method is highly successful.

How might you use the link method in everyday life? Harry Lorayne suggests

> Let's assume that you have the following errands to do on one particular day: You have to have your car washed . . . ; make a deposit at the bank; post a letter; see your dentist; pick up the umbrella that you forgot at a friend's house . . . ; buy some perfume for your wife; call or see the television repair man; stop at the hardware shop . . ." (Lorayne, p. 53)

The imaginary day proceeds with further rounds of errands. (As Harry Lorayne notes, "My, but you've got a busy day!") However, the procedure for ensuring you remember all these items remains quite simple: You simply form visual images of each pair. To connect car wash and bank, for example, visualize yourself driving into your bank in a recently washed car. You then see yourself depositing letters instead of money and picture your dentist pulling letters out of your mouth, and so on.

A number of image-based mnemonic systems have been devised, and they have a variety of different uses. Harry Lorayne promises the readers of his book that when they have mastered the described techniques they will be able to remember a 50-digit number after examining it just once, or recall a 50-item shopping list, or the correct order of a pack of cards. There is no reason to doubt the truth of these claims. However, the methods underlying the more ambitious feats are quite complicated, and learning them takes considerable time and effort.

Consequently, before embarking on the lengthy task of acquiring the method that makes it possible to recall, for instance, the order of a pack of cards, it may be wise to ask yourself whether your desire to perform this feat is strong enough to justify the hours spent in mastering it.

In general, the effects of mnemonic techniques are highly impressive, and they provide excellent demonstrations of the possible benefits of having a good strategy. However, the kinds of learning and remembering improved are usually ones depending upon the acquisition of lists of ordered materials such as words or numbers. Most situations in real life where one wants to remember something are more complicated and untidy: Life varies from the list-learning situations commonly used in mnemonic demonstrations and in memory research. We need to know to what extent methods such as imagery-based mnemonics and other strategies can be applied to practical circumstances in everyday life.

USING IMAGERY IN FOREIGN-LANGUAGE ACQUISITION

Foreign-language acquisition is a practical field of learning where imagery technique is highly successful. Mastering foreign languages is not easy, and the task of learning a large foreign vocabulary is particularly difficult. Most people find the necessary regular study arduous and time consuming, to say the least. A memory strategy organizing or relating items on the basis of shared meanings is not very helpful for vocabulary acquisition, because the relationship between an English word and its foreign equivalent may appear to the learner to be quite arbitrary. By using imagery, however, it is possible to make links between two words in different languages. In consequence, memory is much improved.

The Keyword Method

A highly successful technique was developed by Richard Atkinson and Michael Raugh (Atkinson, 1975; Raugh & Atkinson, 1975; Raugh, Shupbach, & Atkinson, 1977; Pressley, 1977). It is called the *keyword method.* To make a connection between a foreign language word and its English equivalent, two links are formed. The first is achieved by selecting a keyword, which is simply an English word that *sounds* similar to the foreign word.

For example, for the Russian *zvonok* (meaning *bell*), which sounds like "zvan-oak," the English word *oak* is employed as the keyword. Students find it quite easy to learn the connection between a foreign word and the similar-sounding English keyword. Other examples of effective keywords are *pot* for the Spanish word *pato* (pronounced roughly "pot-o"), meaning *duck; top* for the Russian word *tapochkim,* meaning *sandals;* and *whop* for the Russian word *klop,* meaning *bedbug.* Two criteria used for selecting an appropriate keyword are, first, the keyword must sound as similar as possible to part (but not necessarily all) of the foreign word and, second, it should be unique and distinct from all other keywords.

The second stage in learning to connect foreign words with their English equivalents is to establish a link between each keyword and the English word meaning the same as the foreign word. It is at this stage that imagery is introduced. The actual procedure is not unlike that of the rhyme method already described. To cite an example given by Raugh, Shupbach, and Atkinson (1977), let us imagine a student learning the Spanish word *caballo* (pronounced roughly "cob-eye-yo"), meaning *horse.* Having first chosen a keyword (*eye*), the student forms a visual image containing both the keyword and the English word. A possible image, for instance, might contain a horse kicking a giant eye. Having formed the joint image, the student can now easily produce horse whenever eye is provided. Presenting the word *caballo* evokes the similar-sounding *eye*, which evokes an eye and horse image. This tells the student that *horse* is the English equivalent of the Spanish word *caballo*.

In short, the keyword method transforms the task from difficult (remembering an arbitrary connection between two unrelated words) to easier (forming a relationship between items based on sound similarity and another connection based on visual images the learner forms).

Does the keyword system work? It does remove the need to form arbitrary connections, and substitutes readily formed links. On the other hand, the method seems to be somewhat cumbersome. The keyword adds complexity to the learning task; it becomes necessary to make two separate links instead of just one.

Atkinson and his colleagues did a number of comparison studies to test the method's effectiveness. In one experiment (Atkinson, 1975), students learned 120 Russian words—40 words on each of 3 successive days. Some of the students followed the keyword method, the keywords being provided by the experimenter. A computer was used to present the words: Items appeared on a cathode ray tube, and students responded via an attached typewriter keyboard. Students heard the Russian word pronounced 3 times, and simultaneously saw the English translation displayed. The students instructed to use keywords also saw the keyword, but some other students (the control group) did not. Each learning trial finished with a test phase, in which each Russian word was pronounced, and students had to type the English equivalent before the next Russian word, within 15 seconds. Testing conditions were the same for students in the keyword and control groups. The findings for each of the 3 days are shown in Figure 5.2. On each day the keyword condition was substantially more effective, and this superiority was maintained. At the end of the 3-day period a retention test for all 120 items was administered. On this occasion, 72% of the items learned by the keyword method were recalled correctly, compared with 46% of the items learned by control group subjects.

Six weeks later, the students were called back without warning for a further memory test of the 120 Russian words. This time the keyword students recalled 43% of the items, and control group subjects recalled only 28%. In short, the students using the keyword method were much more successful than the other students in both of the final tests. The keyword method was highly effective for helping students in this arduous stage of foreign-language learning.

The keyword method has been shown to be equally successful in a number of experiments using Spanish words. In one study, students who used the method recalled 88% of the English equivalents of Spanish words, while students in a control condition only remembered 28%. (Raugh & Atkinson, 1975). A further study was undertaken to find out whether students engaged in regular language courses would voluntarily use the method, and whether they would continue to exercise it once the

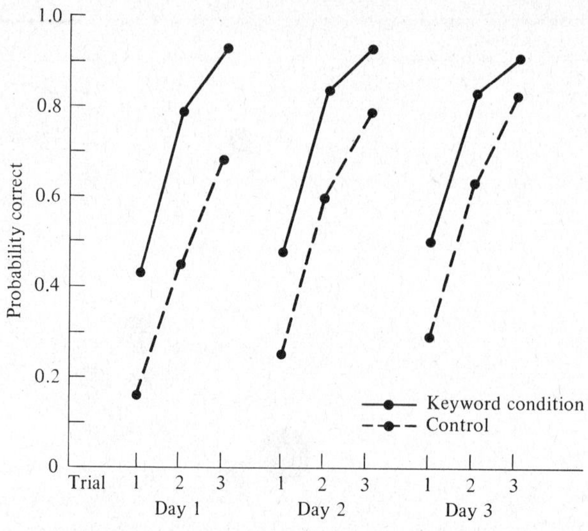

Figure 5.2 Recall of the meanings of Russian words, under keyword and control conditions of learning. *Source:* Atkinson (1975).

novelty wore off. These students were enrolled in a Russian course at Stanford University. They were observed over a 9-week period; during this time span, they attempted to learn about 700 words. Although all the students received instruction in the keyword method, they were entirely free to use it or not to use it, according to personal preference. In fact, these students frequently did choose to use the keyword method.

The probability of a student requesting a keyword (an indication that the method was being used) on a particular trial depended on whether or not the foreign word had been successfully translated on the previous trial. If it had, the probability of a keyword being requested on the second trial was .47. If the correct word was *not* recalled on the first trial, the probability that a keyword would be requested on the next trial rose to .59. Between the first and last weeks there was a large increase in the number of student requests for keywords, showing the method's use was by no means confined to novel circumstances. On the contrary, the more familiar it became the more frequently students used it, except on the first presentation of each new word. At this time, keyword requests were made for around 70% of the words throughout the entire 9-week period.

A Keyword Method for Children

A final question about the keyword method is: Does it work with children? We cannot assume that the answer will be affirmative, for two reasons. First, the method adds to the complexity of learning, and this might make it unsuitable for young children. Secondly, there is evidence that strategies depending upon forming visual images are less effective than alternative strategies with young children. (The difficulties young children have with imagery strategies are not in making images as such, but in transferring from a visual image to a verbal report, and vice versa.) Pressley (1977) designed an experiment to test the keyword method's effectiveness in second and fifth grade children learning Spanish words. To make it easier for the children to use the method, they did not have to make visual images unaided, but were given an imagery link for each item. This was a picture wherein the keyword object and the English word item interacted. The picture was provided in addition to the actual keyword. Processing an image provided in picture form is easier than generating one's own image. Therefore, the keyword method becomes easier to use.

The children learned lists of Spanish words. Second grade children learned 12 words, and older children learned 18 words, all of them nouns. The children using the method were carefully instructed in its use, and their performance was compared with that of other children who were given an equal amount of time to learn the words. When he tested recall, Pressley found that the second grade children using the keyword method recalled around 8 of the 12 words, on average, but the other subjects averaged less than 4 words. Children in the fifth grade who followed the keyword method recalled 11 out of the 18 words, compared with only 6 words recalled by the other children. Clearly, the keyword method was highly successful at both age levels; the children instructed to use it remembered about twice as many items as those who did not.

VISUAL IMAGERY AND LEARNING: EXPERIMENTAL INVESTIGATIONS

Word Concreteness

Prompted by the growing number of experiments demonstrating the effectiveness of visual imagery mnemonic systems, psychologists conducted many other investigations. Their studies provided ample evidence that forming visual images can have a marked beneficial influence (Paivio, 1969). In a number of investigations, Alan Paivio introduced words varying in *concreteness*, a factor he found strongly related to one's ease in forming a visual image. For instance, it is much easier to make an image of a concrete item such as bishop or altar than of an abstract concept such as religion. Paivio suggested that, if imagery contributes to learning, pairs of concrete words should be easier to learn than equally familiar abstract items. In one experiment (Paivio, 1965), participants looked at pairs of either concrete or abstract words. Paivio found that the greatest amount of learning took place when both words were concrete. Pairs containing two abstract words produced the least recall, and mixed pairs, comprised of one concrete and one abstract item, led to intermediate levels of performance.

Further experimental research has been conducted with a view to shedding light on the way word concreteness aids learning. It is conceivable that the improved remembering is not caused by visual imagery as such, but by other factors present when learners form mental images. One possibility is that the degree of the word's association to other word items, as measured by Noble's (1952) associative measure of *meaningfulness,* is the crucial factor—rather than imagery. (Noble rated meaningfulness of words by measuring how effective they were in eliciting related words when shown to subjects who then wrote down any other words that came to mind.) It is known that high-scoring words are often concrete items that are highly imageable, the correlation between meaningfulness and word imageability being +.69. Hence it is possible that the reason Paivio found concrete (highly imageable) words easily learned was not because they readily evoked images, but simply because the words happened to be highly meaningful ones, having numerous word associations.

To test this suggestion, Paivio (1967) presented people with lists of word items that varied in both meaningfulness and concreteness. He found that the correlation between item memory and the ease subjects had in forming images of them was considerably higher than the correlation between remembering and the measure of word meaningfulness. This finding clearly contradicts the view that meaningfulness is the key factor. He also used a technique known as *partial correlation* in order to estimate the extent each of two variables, concreteness and meaningfulness, was related to remembering, once the influence of the other factor was extracted. The correlation between meaningfulness and learning was reduced to +.25, but the correlation between remembering and imageability remained considerably higher—+.47. Furthermore, in an experiment by Paivio, Yuille, and Rogers (1969), imageability and meaningfulness were independently manipulated, and varying the degree of item imageability had a much larger effect upon remembering than varying the item meaningfulness, as Figure 5.3 shows.

Levels of Imagery Processing

Some kinds of visual information are more readily retained and recalled than others, and visual images need not lead to equally accurate recall of all materials. Findings described by J. D. Bransford (1979) indicate that, just as a person's memory for verbal information is influenced by the kind

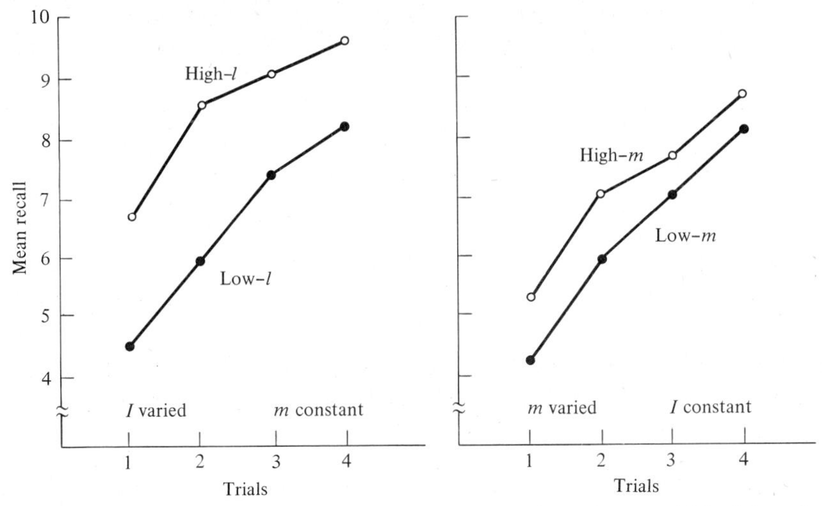

Figure 5.3 Recall scores for words of high and low imageability (*I*) and meaningfulness (*m*). *Source:* Paivio, Yuille, and Rogers (1969).

of input processing taking place (see Chapter 3), memory for pictorial information may also be affected by particular kinds of visual processing activities. In one experiment all the participants were shown the same colored magazine picture of a living room for a period of one minute. All the subjects were instructed to look for objects in the room. Some of the participants (Group 1) were told to scan the picture vertically and horizontally in order to locate some very small inked-in x's. (In fact, there were no x's.) Participants in Group 2 were also instructed to look for x's, but these subjects were told that the x's would be found on the contours of objects in the picture. Group 3 subjects inspected the picture for the same amount of time as the others, but were told to think about the kinds of actions they could perform with the objects depicted. The participants in the fourth group were told they would be asked to form an image of the picture as soon as the inspection period ended.

In fact, after the one-minute period was completed, all participants were asked to imagine the pictured room and recall as much as they could about it. Despite the fact that people in each of the four groups were given an identical amount of time to inspect the picture, there were very large differences in their recall. On average, participants in Groups 3 and 4 recalled around 5 times as many of the pictured items as the other subjects. Clearly, not all visual inspection activities are equally effective. The processing taking place when a person is encouraged to attend to the meaningfully significant aspects of a pictured object (as subjects in Groups 3 and 4 were) leads to much more accurate recall than the inspection activities undertaken by people in Groups 1 and 2, who attended to superficial form and structure. Indeed, differences in the processing undertaken may be as important in determining memory for pictured and visually imaged materials as they are for recall of the verbal materials described in Chapter 3.

IMAGERY AND VISUAL PROCESSES

We do not know exactly how imagery contributes to learning and memory. Research findings indicate that the necessary mental analyses involve coding and processing nonverbal information (Pylyshyn, 1973). In forming mental images we use mechanisms also needed for visual perception. In some circumstances, performing an imagery task interferes with perceptual tasks, and vice versa. For example, in a study by Gordon Bower (1972), people made more mistakes if they performed a visual imagery task and a visual perception task at the same time than if they simultaneously performed a visual imagery task and a perceptual task not involving vision. This finding supports the view that visual imagery and visual perception share mental mechanisms common to both.

Participants in Bower's investigation learned word pairs either by a visual imagery strategy—visualizing scenes containing the two items—or by rote repetition. While learning the words, participants also performed a distracting task. For some subjects this task was visual. They tracked a moving wavy line with their finger. Others were told to close their eyes and also tracked a moving line. In their case the line was a length of string, glued to backing paper, and tracking was purely tactile, involving touch and not vision.

Bower found that people using visual imagery as a learning strategy recalled more words when their distracting task was tactile. They recalled 66% of the words in this condition. When the distracting task involved visual tracking, 55% of the words were recalled. However, the form of the distractor did not influence remembering by people using visual imagery; they remembered 28% of the words, irrespective of the distractor given.

Several other investigators also found that visual imagery and visual perception tasks interfere with each other, supporting the view that they share mechanisms. For example, Segal and Fusella (1969) discovered that having to imagine a visual scene makes it more difficult to detect faint lights. G. Atwood (Bower, 1970) observed that asking people to do a visual task decreased their memory of concrete (highly imageable) words more than abstract words. Performing an auditory task had the opposite effect. However, visual tasks do not interfere with memory of concrete words unless learners are actually making images (Baddeley, Grant, Wight, & Thomson, 1974).

Luria's Report

Imagery played a big role in the life of one individual with an exceptional memory, S. V. Shereshevskii (*S*), whose achievements are described in a short book by the Soviet psychologist A. R. Luria (1968). According to Luria's account, *S* reported that he could remember almost everything he had experienced, and *S*'s performance in a number of memory tests Luria devised was unquestionably phenomenal. For instance, after spending 3 minutes examining a table of 50 numbers, arranged in 4 columns and 13 rows, *S* could not only reproduce all the numbers, but was able to do so in any order that Luria requested: column by column, diagonally, or in a single 50-number sequence. When Luria asked *S* to recall these numbers after an interval of several months, *S* did so without any errors. On a number of instances *S* recalled detailed materials he had learned 15 years previously.

Although *S*'s exceptional memory was useful to him in a number of ways, he did not regard it as an unmixed blessing. *S*, who was a newspaper reporter, said that his inability to forget things was often frustrating and he had great difficulty in thinking abstractly. Luria noted that when *S* tried to read poetry he encountered overwhelming obstacles in understanding. Each expression would give rise to an image that conflicted with previous images.

> How, then, to break through this chaos of images to the poem itself. . . . Many people think that poetry calls for the most graphic kind of thinking. Yet, upon analyzing this idea, it seems most doubtful, for poetry does not evoke images as much as ideas. The images in a poem merely serve to clothe meaning, the underlying intention of a poem. Hence, to understand a poem, we much be able to grasp the figurative meaning suggested by an image. . . . (Luria, 1968, p. 120)

One of *S*'s problems was that *all* his thoughts were accompanied by intense visual images, which sometimes conflicted with the meaning of prose descriptions, as well as poetry. His ability to remember something depended upon his forming a mental image of it. *S* reported that he formed visual images in a variety of circumstances and that the act of remembering took the form of "reading" from a clear visual image.

He said that he could *see* whatever he was recalling; therefore, the order in which items had to be reported made no difference at all. When *S* was asked to remember something, he first had to bring to mind the occasion where he had originally perceived the required item. Once that occasion had been reevoked, *S* would have a strong visual image at hand, and he simply read off the items requested.

Luria's detailed description of a man with an exceptional ability to remember, depending heavily on images, is quite unique. However, there are other people in whom extraordinary memory accomplishments are accompanied by intense imagery. For instance, Colthart and Glick (1974) describe a young woman who formed strong visual images of the letters in sentences. When examined at age 22, she could read from these images and could spell the letters backwards at great speed. But her memory for nonverbal visual materials and scenes was not remarkable, and her ability to visualize words was no help to her in life.

Eidetic Imagery

Unusual forms of remembering dependent upon imagery are also encountered in young children who make *eidetic images.* The belief that some people have *photographic memory* receives some support from the finding (Haber & Haber, 1964) that around 8% of young children can retain accurate literal reproductions of visual scenes they see.

In memory tests, these children, who are known as eidetic imagers, can read off the contents of these images. This results in detailed recall of particular items, apparently without any sophisticated retrieval strategy. The literal "photographic" image retained can enable a child to report each of the items in a long word, for instance, even though the child cannot read. The images are usually very clear and last for at least half a minute.

The eidetic images that some children experience are quite different from images made by other people. Children who are recalling from an eidetic image always speak of the items as if they are still present rather than being deliberately remembered. (In this respect eidetic imagers are similar to *S.*) Furthermore, recall is accompanied by the same eye-scanning movements that a child makes when the object is actually present.

Eidetic images' practical contribution is disappointing. Eidetic imagers cannot use their apparently valuable gift in any useful way. Indeed, eidetic imagery is four times as common in mentally retarded children as in normal children. This fact leads one to suspect that, despite its apparent impressiveness, memory dependent upon eidetic imagery is in reality a primitive memory mechanism having a useful function only in the earliest years of life, if at all. It perhaps aids retention of visual information in a relatively unprocessed form.

Whatever its role in early development, eidetic imagery in most children is soon superseded by representative abilities that are less literal and depend on more extensive processing. As we know, intelligent human behavior depends upon one's ability to store and retrieve the meaning of things, and this is not possible with a photographic record.

Professor Aitken

Although exceptional memory may be accompanied by unusual reliance upon imagery, as in the cases of *S* and the young woman described by Colthart and Glick, not everyone who is exceptionally good at remembering depends upon imagery to an unusual extent. One instance was a professor of mathematics, A. C. Aitken, whose remarkable achievements at remembering numbers and performing difficult mental calculations were described by Ian Hunter (1962; 1977). Aitken's memory feats included reciting the value of pi (π) to a thousand decimal places. He possessed an amazing amount of knowledge about numbers and number relationships, and this knowledge both depended upon and contributed to his memory. Thus, on hearing the sequence 1961, Aitken immediately recognized it as being the sum of $44^2 + 5^2$ or $40^2 + 19^2$, and the product of 37×53. Partly because his remembering was linked to a body of highly organized abstract knowledge, Aitken, unlike *S*, made good use of his memory skills by performing practical feats of mental calculation and problem solving.

Chapter 6
Retrieval

FINDING INFORMATION STORED IN MEMORY

To remember something, it is not only necessary to store it in memory: A person also has to *find* the stored item. If a store contains a very large number of items, locating the particular one sought may present serious problems. As I noted in Chapter 2, this was a reason for rejecting the theory that human memory operates on the principles of a simple chest of drawers: Searching through the numerous stored materials in order to locate and retrieve the required ones would take far too long. An efficient memory, or any other system dealing with the problems involved in storing numerous different items, must make effective provision for location of any of the retained materials. As we have seen, a factor influencing the degree of access to retained materials is their *organization.* In libraries, for instance, access to large quantities of books is improved by careful organization, in conjunction with cataloging facilities.

An item's retention in memory does not guarantee ability to actually recall it. Item recall depends in part upon the circumstances at the time remembering is tested. For example, we find it easier to recognize something than to recall it. Why should this be?

The superiority of recognition over recall is partly due to differences in the necessary retrieval operations. In order to either recognize or recall an item, it is essential to retain some description of that item in memory. In a recognition test, the task of locating or identifying information stored in memory is a relatively easy one. In effect, one simply has to decide whether something in memory corresponds with or matches an item shown in the recognition test. In a test of recall, on the other hand, the individual has to perform a more active search. Rather than simply having to locate something matching a provided item, one has the additional problem of having to decide exactly what to look for. Recognition tests do not eliminate the retrieval needs, but they do simplify the retrieval task. In general, experimental findings confirm the commonsense belief that recognition is easier than recall.

Sometimes, when we cannot recall something, we nevertheless have a strong feeling that it is stored in memory. We feel the particular item is available in memory, but not accessible, despite our efforts to retrieve it. For instance, when I am asked to name an acquaintance, I may fail to remember the name, but remain convinced that I do know it. I have a strong "feeling of knowing" the name (Hart, 1967); or, the name for which I am searching seems to be "on the tip of the tongue" (Brown & McNeill, 1966).

Research has confirmed that the apparent awareness of materials retained in memory, despite inability to gain access, is often a realistic indication of the true state of affairs. Accuracy of these feeling of knowing experiences was assessed in a study in which people tried to answer questions of general knowledge (Hart, 1965). When a person could *not* give the right answer to a question he was told to check "No" if he simply did not know the answer, or "Yes" if he felt he did know the answer, even though he could not provide it immediately. Subsequently, there was a recognition test containing all those items not recalled. Hart wanted to discover if those items a person had responded positively to would be more frequently identified than items to which the person had responded "No." He found that people recognized 76% of the answers they had reported having a feeling of knowing, on average; they recognized only 43% of the "No" items.

Clearly, a person's feelings of knowing something do provide valid information about the availability in memory of information temporarily inaccessible to recall tests. Of course, the fact that someone cannot recall an item on one occasion does not mean he will never remember it: Often, items that cannot be recalled at one time are remembered later (Patterson, 1972; Tulving & Pearlstone, 1966).

Some further evidence about locating information stored in memory was obtained in an experiment by Brown and McNeill (1966). They read aloud some definitions of unusual English words and the participants had to name the word. Quite often, as in the previous study, a person would report that although he could not name a particular item, he did have a feeling of knowing it, or it was on the tip of his tongue. Brown and McNeill were interested in discovering if people did know something about those words they could not immediately reproduce. Participants were shown a list of 49 words, and were told to select the ones that *sounded* closest to and furthest from the correct one, and also those most similar and most dissimilar in *meaning*. The participants' choices revealed that they did indeed have some knowledge of the meaning and sound of words they could not remember. Again, it appears that people can retrieve *some* information about inaccessible items.

Comparing Recall and Recognition

People may recognize far more than they can recall. Recognition memory for pictures is especially remarkable. In one study, students looked at over 2,500 slides for 10 seconds each (Standing, Conezio, & Haber, 1970). Most of the slides contained vacation scenes and it took 4 daily 2-hour sessions to view all of them. Later, the students were shown pairs of slides consisting of a new one and one that had been shown previously. The task was to identify the familiar slide. About 90% of the subjects' choices were correct. Shepard (1967) and Howe (1967b) also observed that people were remarkably successful at recognizing items from lengthy sequences of pictures. Shepard found that people were also very good at recognizing sentences, even a week after seeing them.

When recognition and recall are directly compared, it is usually found that people recognize more items than they recall. In a typical study, after 5 presentations of a list of 100 words, people recalled on average only 38, but recognized 96 (Mandler, Pearlstone, & Koopmans, 1969). But recognition success is reduced if the recognition test contains large numbers of incorrect distractor items (Davis, Sutherland, & Judd, 1961) or if the incorrect items are similar to the correct ones (Dale & Baddeley, 1962).

In some circumstances, recognition is actually inferior to recall. J. McNulty (1966) has suggested that people are normally better at recognition than recall because it is often possible to recognize something when one's memory is incomplete, if *part* of the information is remembered. When the incorrect items in a recognition test are highly similar to the correct ones, a subject whose memory is incomplete cannot discriminate between the correct item and other ones. Consequently, performance at recognizing is no better than recall, and sometimes worse (Bahrick & Bahrick, 1964; Bruce & Cofer, 1965).

HOW INFORMATION IS LOCATED

In order to recall something, it has to be located among the numerous other materials stored in memory. As in other search situations, the chance of an item's successful retrieval from memory depends upon, among other things, the detailed information available about the required item's nature, and about its possible location. Various kinds of information can serve as clues or cues to help people locate information in memory.

One way to cue recall is to provide an item similar or related to the one we are looking for. Then materials are retained in memory in a highly organized manner, on the basis of meaningful attributes. Items sharing meanings in common are said to be *close* to each other in semantic memory—in something like the sense that two library books on the same topic are close to one another in a library catalog (Collins & Loftus, 1975). Closeness refers simply to case of access between items, and need not correspond with physical proximity.

The activities of high school students in an investigation by Tulving and Pearlstone (1966) give substance to the above account. The students heard lists containing words belonging to a number of categories. Subsequently, half the students were asked simply to recall the words. The others were given cues at the time of recall, in the form of the original category headings, which were announced one at a time. After hearing each category there was an interval of time for recall before subjects heard the next category label. These students recalled more items than the first group, irrespective of the length of the list and the number of words in each category. Students who heard the category headings provided as recall cues were directed toward the words they sought.

Input Processing and Retrieval

It is time to go into a little more detail about the relationship between remembering and processing occurring at time of input. In Chapter 3 I suggested that items processed at input in a way that provides descriptions of their *meanings* are especially likely to be retrievable. A stored description designating an item's meaning is more likely to be unique in memory, and hence more *distinctive,* than an item description that specifies, say, the color or the sound of an item. However, I also noted that in some instances, item descriptions specifying structural characteristics can also be highly distinctive, and hence easy to locate—just as a library book bound in gold is distinctive if all the other volumes are blue or red.

According to Craik and Lockhart (1972) the *depth* of input processing is an especially important influence upon remembering. By deep processing, they meant the (probably extensive) perceptual processing necessary to analyze an event's meaning, resulting in a description of the meaning being retained in memory. They believed perceptual processing of physical characteristics was achieved by *shallower,* less extensive input processing. Roughly speaking, the deeper the mental processing, the more abstract and meaningful the level of input analysis, and the corresponding memory traces formed.

Up to a point, this is a fair account of the differences in input processing that influence memory. However, a number of critics noticed that Craik and Lockhart were rather vague in stating what they meant by depth of processing. It is not clear precisely how deep input processing differs from that leading to shallow levels of analysis. It is reasonable to suggest that the processing that produces a memory trace describing an event's meaning must be more complicated, elaborate, or extensive than that required to provide a physical description. However, the dimension of depth may be inadequate for describing what is actually different about the processing. Furthermore, depth implies a continuous variable, suggesting that the processing necessary for a meaningful analysis may be simply "more of the same" processing necessary for a physical analysis. In reality, it is more likely that meaningful analysis requires fundamentally different forms of input processing.

To be fair, the authors of the depth of processing view were aware of this problem and did not intend the concept of depth to provide more than a rough indication of the nature of the differences in mental processing. They were more concerned, at first, simply to draw attention to the influence of differences in perceptual processing.

They attempted to add precision to the levels approach by suggesting that processing also varies in *degree of elaboration.* This affects the precision with which remembered events are described by memory traces. Also, Jacoby, Craik, and Begg (1979) stressed the importance of the *distinctiveness* of encoded descriptions as a recognition factor. They say:

> [M]ore extensive analysis is reflected in a richer, more distinctive memory record of the event. The distinctive record, in turn, is highly discriminable from other memory traces and is retrieved with apparent ease. (Jacoby, Craik, & Begg, 1979, p. 596)

I have already said that there are a number of ways of making a memory trace distinctive. Remembering is affected not by input processing alone, but by the extent to which input processing analysis forms a discriminable memory description. A discriminable description is distinctive, readily located, and easily retrieved. Furthermore, the distinctiveness of a memory trace, when one is trying to remember something, depends not only on the previous input processing but also upon the circumstances at the time of recall. Jacoby, Craik, and Begg point out that distinctiveness, unlike the elaboration of a memory trace, can only be assessed by taking into account both study conditions and testing conditions. Particularly important is the relationship, or degree of correspondence, between the two—between the processing occurring at input and the particular circumstances existing during retrieval attempts. If there is some kind of match between input processing and, say, word cues provided to help recall, accurate memory is highly likely. For instance, if an event is processed at input on the basis of a meaningful quality, and during retrieval one is given cues in the form of a word having the same meaning, the cue word will be effective for locating the stored item. In this case, a word cue directs the person's memory search to the appropriate place.

ENCODING SPECIFICITY

The importance of the match between input processing and retrieval circumstances is illustrated by the findings of an experiment by Tulving and Thomson (1973). Students had to remember words. When each word was presented, it was accompanied by another word that shared a meaning with it.

As you know, many words have more than one meaning. When a word is presented along with another word of similar meaning, the meaningful input analysis of the to-be-remembered word produces a memory trace referring to the meaning shared between the two words. For instance, if *ball* is accompanied by *gown* we would expect the memory trace to describe qualities of *ball* that concern dancing and festivities, rather than team sports or any other meaning. Consequently, if a word is to be given as a retrieval cue at the time that a person tries to remember *ball*, the most effective cue will be the very same item that accompanied presentation. This is because the meaning it evokes is the one described in the memory trace. The word *game*, on the other hand, would not be a good retrieval cue because although *game* is undoubtedly related to *ball*, it does not share the meaning earlier analyzed. Therefore, it does not provide easier access to the memory trace, which describes the shared meaning of *ball* and *gown*.

In short, an effective retrieval cue must not simply direct the person to any meaning of the stored item but to the particular meaning actually encoded in the memory trace. An effective retrieval cue will guide the individual toward that area of organized memory (or *semantic space*) where the memory trace representing the required information can be found.

To serve as an effective retrieval cue, an item may not have to be identical to one that accompanied presentation of the information being remembered. What is important is that the retrieval cue directs the person to the same meaning. If we give the retrieval cue *dance* to someone trying to remember *ball*, which was accompanied by *gown*, the retrieval cue would be helpful. Although the word is a new one, the meaning is similar.

Note that in order to accurately predict whether something will be remembered or not, we must not only know how the person has processed the information, but also what cues are available to help retrieval. To make a good prediction, it is important to know *both* these things, so that the match between input and recall conditions can be assessed.

The findings of experimental research support and add substance to the above description of input and retrieval operations. Tulving and Osler (1968) found that words related to a to-be-remembered item of information might be ineffective as retrieval cues if they had not been present during perception. These authors concluded that for a word to function as a retrieval cue it was necessary to store information about the relationship between the cue and the remembered word at the same time as the word was processed.

Similar effects with recognition memory were observed by Light and Carter-Sobell (1970). They found that if a noun was presented together with a qualifying adjective (such as *strawberry* and *jam*), presenting the original adjective in a subsequent recognition test led to 67% correct recognition. However, with a new adjective having a different meaning (*traffic*), only 27% of the items were recognized. For this reason, Reder, Anderson, and Bjork (1974) found that related words not present at the same time as a to-be-remembered item were most likely to cue recall of the item if the precise meaning of the latter was encoded at the time of presentation and not greatly influenced by the context. (The word *rhinoceros* provides an instance of a word whose meaning is not much affected by its linguistic context.)

Encoding specificity effects also occur when people read sentences (Barclay, Bransford, Franks, McCarell, & Nitsch, 1974). After reading the word *ink* in a number of different sentences, such as:

The student spilled the ink.
The student picked up the ink.

Subjects were given recall cues that either did or did not match the meaning of the sentence. For the above sentences, the cues were:

Something in a bottle.
Something messy.

Cue words directing a participant's retrieval attempts to the original contextual meaning of the word produced correct recall of the item three times as frequently as did cues indicating a different meaning.

KNOWLEDGE AND RETRIEVAL

If a word presented at the same time as the item to be remembered is to influence that word's encoding, it is essential that one actually knows the meaning implied by the word pair. Otherwise, the word would be processed just as if it had been presented on its own. In the latter case a retrieval cue word with a different meaning than that of the original word pair may nevertheless direct the individual to the right item.

It follows that in certain circumstances, the greater a person's knowledge about words and their meanings, the *fewer* the items they will recall. By way of illustration, consider the situation in which two children are both given the input pair *ankle-calf*. The older child understands the relationship between the two; therefore, she processes and codes a memory trace referring to parts of the body.

The second child is ignorant of any meaningful relationship between *ankle* and *calf;* therefore, when presented with the word *calf* she does not process it in a way reflecting that particular meaning. Now suppose that at recall time, the word *cow* is given as a cue. It is quite likely that *cow* will direct the younger child to the meaning of *calf* stored in her memory. For the older child, however, *cow* will clearly not lead toward the stored memory trace produced when *ankle* and *calf* occurred together. As a result, there is a higher probability that the younger child will be successful in remembering the correct word.

Does it actually happen? Precisely this occurred in an experiment by Ceci and Howe (1978a). In circumstances like the ones outlined, younger children consistently recalled considerably more words than older participants. Children's memory was tested in a condition where the meaning of the word used as a retrieval cue was different (incompatible) from the meaning of the input pair. Young children who *did* know a meaning of the to-be-remembered word but did *not* know the particular meaning shared by the input pair consistently remembered more words than the older children, who knew both the different (incompatible) meanings. This finding is depicted in Figure 6.1.

When input pairs and output cues have incompatible meanings, children having sufficient word-meaning knowledge to retain memory traces incompatible with recall cue words remember fewer words than younger children who lack such knowledge. When both older and youn-

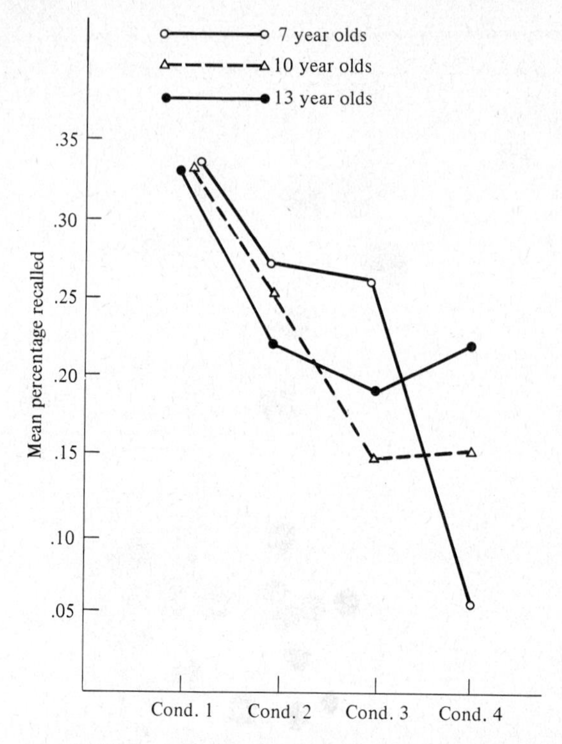

Figure 6.1 Mean percentage of words that were correctly recalled as a function of condition. Condition 1 (knowledge compatible for all ages). Condition 2 (knowledge compatible for 13-year-olds but no knowledge incompatible for 7- and 10-year-olds). Condition 3 (knowledge incompatible for 10- and 13-year-olds but no knowledge incompatible for 7-year-olds), and Condition 4 (knowledge incompatible for all ages). *Source:* Ceci and Howe (1978a).

ger children possess the relevant knowledge, older children do better than younger subjects.

RETRIEVAL STRATEGIES

We have seen that the likelihood of a stored item actually being recalled is affected by three things: the kind of input processing it receives, the information provided at the time of recall (for example, a related word serving as a recall cue), and the correspondence or match between these factors. Another influence on remembering is the degree of resourcefulness going into the memory search undertaken to locate stored information. Whenever one looks for something, an intelligent, flexible, and adaptable search is more likely to yield the desired result than a narrow and inflexible search. This statement applies to the memory searching operations leading to items being retrieved, as is demonstrated by the findings of a further investigation by Ceci and Howe (1978b).

In the study I have just described, Ceci and Howe found that there was one condition where older children recalled appreciably more items than younger children. In this condition, all the children knew enough about the words to understand the meanings of both the input and output (recall cue) word pairs, but, at the same time, the input and output words suggested different meanings of the word to be remembered. (An example: the input pair was *pay-bill* and the recall cue was *bird*.) A likely explanation is that when the memory search process initiated by the (incompatible) recall cue fails to locate the actual word, older subjects are more resourceful and flexible in generating alternative strategies to redirect their search. Ceci and Howe next designed an experiment in which children could improve their recall by using a flexible retrieval strategy. Consider the following words:

stagecoach
buffalo
cowboy
rickshaw
ox
mandarin
land-rover
camel
belly-dancer

These are some of the items from a list of 24 that were presented to a number of children. On inspecting the list you may notice that they can be grouped in either of two ways. First, they form a number of separate *taxonomic classes:*

Travel (*stagecoach, rickshaw, land-rover*)
Animals (*buffalo, ox, camel*)
People (*cowboy, mandarin, belly-dancer*)

Alternatively, it is possible to group the same list of words into a number of different *themes:*

The Wild West (*stagecoach, buffalo, cowboy*)
The Orient (*rickshaw, ox, mandarin*)
The Desert (*land-rover, camel, belly-dancer*)

All the children were shown how to categorize the items into taxonomic groups and also shown how to group the items according to theme. The experimenter made quite sure that every child could perform both types of organization.

Later, the children tried to remember the words they had studied.

In attempting recall it helps to use the groupings (either taxonomic, thematic, or both): These provide good cues to help retrieve the individual words from memory. One child might use a retrieval strategy relying exclusively on either one of two alternative grouping methods; for example, she might think first of "People" and remember the word in that category, and then go on to "Animals" and "Travel," remaining all the while within the taxonomic mode of classification. She need never switch from the taxonomic grouping to the thematic categorization. Another child's recall strategy might depend entirely upon the cues provided by the thematic groupings. This child might start with the words in "The Wild West" and then proceed to "The Orient" and "The Desert." The second child relies exclusively on the thematic groupings to give cues for aiding retrieval, and never switches to the taxonomic groups.

A third child might adopt a more flexible recall strategy. When this child is trying to remember the items, he not only proceeds from one group to the next (for example, "People," "Travel," "Animals," and so on) within one of the two modes: He also switches *between* modes when it is useful. That is, he switches from the taxonomic to the thematic groupings, and vice versa. For example, having exhausted all the words he recalls from the taxonomic categories, he might then try using the thematic group headings as cues for recalling additional words stored in memory but not yet recalled. In this way, a greater number of potentially fruitful retrieval cues are available. As a result, it is likely more items will be recalled.

Older children often behave more flexibly and adaptively than young children. Ceci and Howe (1978b) posited that if children were trying to remember words from lists like the one just described, older children would adopt more flexible recall strategies. It was predicted that inspection of the records showing each child's recall order would reveal that when trying to remember the words, older children would make more switches between the two different modes of classification. It was also predicted that, largely as a result of their more flexible recall strategies, the older children would remember more items than the younger.

Both of these predictions were confirmed. In fact, 10-year-olds switched between the 2 modes more than twice as often as 7-year-olds and 4 times as often as 4-year-olds. Among the 4-year-olds, in all 60 instances where successive words came from different groups, only 9 of the changes between groups involved a switch between the thematic and taxonomic modes. In 10-year-olds, by contrast, 38 of such instances involved a switch between modes. The older children's more flexible retrieval strategies were paralleled by considerably more accurate recall. Four-year-olds recalled 12.25 of the 25 items, on average; 7-year-olds' recall averaged 16.75 items; and 10-year-olds recalled 18.5 words. Of course, the relation of recall accuracy and flexible retrieval strategy does not, in itself, prove that retrieval flexibility actually *caused* better memory. However, a further analysis of the data, using the reduction method of Tulving and Watkins (1975), assessed the extent that items not remembered in the free recall test had actually been retained. The analysis indicated that the older children did not actually retain much more information than the younger subjects. The older subjects' superior recall was largely due to their adopting more flexible retrieval strategies.

Differences in the strategies people use to search for items retained in memory contribute to individual differences in remembering, and to the differences in recall found when young and older children are compared. Recall is most accurate when the retrieval strategies one uses are closely meshed with or matched to the processes of perceptual input analysis and the initially stored description. Differences in skill at co-ordinating input processing and retrieval activities may make a definite contribution to individual variability in what people can remember.

Chapter 7
Knowing and Remembering

Look at the following sentence:

"The policeman held up his hand and stopped the car."

What does it mean? The phrase "held up his hand" *could* mean that the policeman grasped one of his own hands and lifted it up, or that he lifted the hand of a suspect. "Stopped the car" *could* indicate that, like Wonder Woman, the policeman exerted enormous strength and literally forced a moving car to a halt.

But you and I know that it is most unlikely that the writer intended to communicate either of these meanings. Why? There is nothing in the sentence itself to contradict them. What is it that makes us interpret the phrases differently?

The answer lies in the knowledge that we, the readers of the sentence, already possess (Collins & Quillian, 1972). When we see "The policeman held up his hand and stopped the car," we comprehend it by making use of our existing knowledge about the world, our organized long-term memory store of information.

This knowledge tells us which of the possible meanings of "held up his hand" and "stopped the car" are the most likely ones in the context of the present sentence. Had we seen the identical phrases in different contexts, our interpretation of them would differ markedly. For example:

"Jack damaged his finger. The doctor held up his hand and examined the injury."

or

"The charging elephant stopped the car."

Both of these examples indicate different meanings than the ones acceptable in the previous sentence. Again, it is the organized knowledge that each person possesses, the contents of long-term memory, making it possible to use contextual information and interpret the identical phrases differently.

THE VALUE OF PRIOR KNOWLEDGE

The knowledge that one acquires has an enormous influence upon what is comprehended and remembered. Psychologists are interested in discovering how the vast store of meaningful knowledge that each person possesses (*semantic memory*) is actually organized and retained in the human brain. A related problem is to find out how people are able to use their own knowledge in order to comprehend, learn from, and remember things they experience.

When you remember events that happened a long time ago, you do not recall a literal carbon copy of the original experience. Long-term remembering is a much more active process. Typically, when you remember a distant event, a degree of *inference* is involved. Without being aware of it, you bring in your background knowledge in order to fill in gaps in literal memory: You partly infer what must have been originally perceived. Some illustrations will show how the inferences one makes contribute to remembering. First, imagine seeing or hearing a sentence in a situation where you are asked to say whether you recognize it as being one that was presented to you earlier. In many instances you would have little difficulty in either recognizing the old sentence or noticing that it is a new one. But in some circumstances, making this decision is much more difficult. If the detailed form of the sentence is new, but the meaningful content is familiar, people find it very difficult to say whether or not the particular sentence was presented earlier. Consider the following:

The elves are tiny.
The elves live under the bridge.
The bridge is made of wood.
The elves drink tea.

The ideas in these four sentences can be combined in various ways. For instance, the single sentence "The tiny elves who live under the wooden bridge drink tea" combines all four ideas. Bransford and Franks (1971) constructed a number of sentences, each of which combined some but not all of the ideas. After people had seen a number of sentences, they saw them again, mixed with some new ones. The subjects had to say which ones they had seen before. The findings showed that if a new sentence shown in the recognition test contained previously presented information, the sentence was often judged to have been presented earlier. Clearly, the subjects were not remembering the exact sentences, but were retaining the meaning. When a new item had the same meaning as previous ones, the participants were unable to identify it as a new sentence. This result supports the statement that we do not retain literal copies of everything we have experienced: We retain essential meanings, enabling us to *reconstruct* our original perceptions.

When we recognize a meaningful description as being familiar, we do not do so by matching the description with a copy retained in memory. Rather, we match the new item against our knowledge about the content. If the new event is consistent with what we know to be true, we are likely to regard it as being familiar. Bransford and Franks asked people to listen to the following sentence:

Three turtles rested beside a floating log, and a fish swam beneath them.

After a number of sentences had been presented, participants were asked whether the ones they had heard included the following:

Three turtles rested on a floating log, and a fish swam beneath it.

The subjects were able to say that this sentence had not appeared before, because the meaning is not consistent with that of the first sentence. However, some people had originally been given a different sentence:

Three turtles rested on a floating log, and a fish swam beneath them.

They believed the new sentence was familiar. Although the sentences are actually different, the information provided in the second one does not clash with the contents of the original sentence. However, this same group was able to reject a sentence containing meaningful content different than that of the original sentence. For instance, they were able to say that the following sentence had not been presented earlier:

Three turtles rested beside a floating log, and a fish swam beneath it.

Our ability to make use of our general knowledge to help remember experienced events is extremely valuable, but it can sometimes lead us astray. We often use background knowledge automatically, without deliberate intention; thus, we cannot always be sure if something recalled is exactly what was presented to us, or a reconstruction inferred from background knowledge about the presented material. Imagine that on Wednesday you read one version of a story already familiar to you. On Thursday you are asked to look at another version of the same story, and to identify the particular detailed content presented in Wednesday's version. In situations like this, people find it very difficult to discriminate between their existing knowledge and closely related recent information. In one experiment (Kintsch, 1975) people read passages about topics that were already familiar to them, such as the Biblical story of Joseph and his brothers. Twenty-four hours later they were quite unable to distinguish between what they had read in the particular passage and their background knowledge of the story.

CONFUSION, WRONG INFERENCES, AND FORGETTING

In some instances, a person's inability to distinguish between recent information and background knowledge can have unfortunate practical consequences. New information broadly consistent with what we already remember can mislead our reconstructive memory processes. One situation where this happens is in court. Witnesses are questioned about an event that occurred some time previously, such as a driving accident. In a study investigating the accuracy of eyewitness testimony, Loftus and Palmer (1974) first showed people a film of a traffic accident. Later, the participants were told to say how fast the vehicles had been moving. Some participants were asked how fast the cars were going when they smashed into each other; others were asked how fast the cars were going when they hit each other. The reported estimates of speed were influenced by the questions. Those people who were asked about the velocity of cars that "smashed into" each other reported a higher average speed than the other participants.

This finding suggests that the nature of the questions may have influenced memory. To confirm this, the participants were asked further questions, such as whether they saw any broken glass. In fact, in the film of the accident there was no broken glass at all. However, some people replied "Yes" to this question, and those whose earlier question included the word "smashed" responded positively more often than the others. The evidence strongly suggests that information supplied *after* an event may indeed influence, and in the present case, dangerously distort, a person's memory for events.

Predicting Distortions in Memory

Memory for information about people's lives can be affected by our prejudices and social stereotypes. Students are better at remembering information about unfavorable behavior (for example, spreading rumors that a roommate is dishonest, or having affairs while married) committed by people unlike themselves than at remembering similar behavior by people like themselves (Howard & Rothhart, 1980). Often, prejudices influence how people *perceive* the same event, but memory is affected even when there is no opportunity for prejudice to influence a person's perceptions of things. In one study, university students read a 750-word passage about the life of a woman named Betty. After learning about Betty's childhood, home life, relationships with parents, and other matters, most of the students were given some further information. Some were told that Betty now lives as a lesbian; others were told that she has a heterosexual life-style.

The authors (Snyder & Uranowitz, 1978) wished to discover whether the subsequent information, which touches people's stereotyped beliefs about homosexuals, would affect students' memory of the information already received. To test recall of Betty's life history, the students were given 36 multiple-choice questions one week after reading the passage about her life. Some of the questions concerned Betty's attitudes toward males and females. For instance:

In high school, Betty
(a) occasionally dated men
(b) never went out with men
(c) went steady
(d) no information provided

What the students actually remembered was strongly affected by the information given after the main passage. For example, people who had read that Betty was a lesbian were more likely to recall (incorrectly) that she never went out with men, and students who read that she had a heterosexual life-style more frequently recalled that she "went steady." In fact, the correct answer is (a); she "occasionally dated men."

The result demonstrates that our beliefs about others have some important consequences. The authors cite a fictional instance: someone one has known since childhood is discovered to have deceived people and behaved criminally. After getting this new information, one's knowledge of the person's life history "may be selectively rewritten to support our current interpretation of his character" (Snyder & Uranowitz, 1978, p. 941). Having labeled him a con artist, they note:

> . . . it may be all too easy to bring to mind a variety of behaviors and incidents that may have been insufficient in themselves to warrant such an interpretation but that, in the light of our current knowledge, do seem to support an inference of psychopathic criminality. (Snyder & Uranowitz, 1978, p. 941)

In trying to see other people as stable and predictable, we create in our minds a world where wrong inferences about others perpetuate themselves. The authors suggest that this is a reason why many widely held stereotypes are resistant to change.

When people are given information, what they remember of it may also be affected by their motives and their reasons for being interested in the information. Two groups of students read the same story, which included details of a house. However, they read it from different perspectives, either from that of a burglar, or from that of a potential house buyer (Pichert & Anderson, 1977). The students' recall of the story was strongly influenced by their perspective. The "buyers" were likely to remember that the roof leaked, for instance, whereas the "burglars" more frequently recalled that there was a color television set.

It is quite possible that when people remember things in everyday life they make considerably more inferences from previous knowledge than the above studies indicate. In most memory experiments, participants make a deliberate effort to remember things as accurately as possible. By contrast, when people normally remember events in many real circumstances, they do so without making any deliberate decision or effort to remember. In a study by Spiro (1980), students were asked to read a story about the problems encountered in the personal relationship between two young people engaged to be married. In one version the couple, Bob and Margie, discover they have a fundamental disagreement. Bob does not ever want to have children; Margie wants very much to have children. Subsequently, some readers were informed that Bob and Margie broke off the engagement and have not seen each other since. Other readers were told they did get married and are still living together happily. Clearly, for the second group of readers, but not the first group, there was an element of imbalance.

Some of the students were told to read the story and report their reactions to it. If the story led to inferences clashing with their own existing knowledge, these elements tended to be recalled erroneously when the participants subsequently recalled the story. They made *accommodative* errors that reduced the discord between the story content and their own existing knowledge.

For example, students who learned that the couple did get married tended to forget or minimize their disagreement about having children. However, another group of students, who were told that their main task was to *remember* the passage, recalled the discordant parts much more accurately. In another study (Ceci, Caves, & Howe, 1980), children listened to a story depicting well-known television and film characters acting in ways discordant with the children's knowledge and expectations. For example, the "Six Million Dollar Man" was described as being too weak to carry a can of paint. Immediate story memory was very accurate. However, if the children were asked some weeks later to recall the characters' behavior in the story, recall was highly inaccurate. The characters' actions as described showed considerable drift toward the children's prior knowledge of them. This result suggests that, in the absence of complete recall, the children unconsciously made inferences about the characters on the basis of their existing knowledge.

These demonstrations show that adults and children process new materials to make them consistent with what they already know. It might be possible to predict what kinds of inferences people will make while trying to remember material without a complete literal retention. If we are aware of what a person already knows in relation to new information he perceives, we can predict not only what he will forget, but also the direction and form of the memory distortions that will occur.

USING ORGANIZED KNOWLEDGE

One way our background knowledge helps us to understand and remember is by providing structures or frameworks of organized knowledge helping us connect and organize new events. Such structures are sometimes known as *schemes* (Bartlett, 1932; Pichert & Anderson, 1978), *scripts* (Schank & Abelson, 1977) or *frames* (Minsky, 1975). They provide ways of using elements common to other events to reduce the load on human memory. That is,

> As an economy measure in the storage of episodes, when enough of them are alike they are remembered in terms of a standardized, generalized episode which we will call a script. (Schank & Abelson, 1977, p. 19)

Look at this little story:

John went to a restaurant. He asked the waitress for coq au vin. He paid the check and left.

So far as it goes, the account is perfectly meaningful. But Schank and Abelson point out that it actually omits a great deal. It does not say, for instance, whether John found a free table in the restaurant, or if he sat down. It does not specify if John had anything to drink with his meal, or whether he had a dessert. It does not go into any detail about where John's table was situated, or how the meal was eaten. Presumably John used a plate, and a knife and fork, but the story does not say so. Nor does it say how John paid for his meal. Did he use cash or a credit card? If the former, did he require change? Did he leave a tip, and if so, for how much? Presumably, someone had to cook the meal, and presumably John ate it, but the account does not actually say so. When John finished eating (assuming he did so), did he immediately leave the restaurant, or did he stay for an hour, drinking coffee? Was he alone, or did he have a partner?

Despite the extreme brevity of the story, most people who read it and are familiar with restaurants feel they can answer most of the numerous questions I have raised. Yes, he did eat the food, he did use a plate (and a knife and fork), and he was most probably unaccompanied. It is possible to answer these questions because it is not necessary to depend entirely upon the brief story: Readers can make use of their own knowledge, in the form of what Schank and Abelson would call a script about going to a restaurant. When one visits a restaurant there is a relatively unchanging routine pattern of events; one can take it for granted that these are likely to occur on most restaurant visits. Therefore, when one reads the story about John, a "going to a restaurant" script is activated, which gives the background structure. If a person tells a story containing a familiar script, it is not necessary to include all the details: The storyteller can assume that readers or listeners will be familiar with the script structure. Indeed, people would be bored by a story that included all these details. We would not normally want to read:

John went into the restaurant. He lifted one leg, and then the other, pushed open the door and went inside. He turned slightly to the left, walked four paces, and spoke to the waiter. . . . Then he followed the waiter for another six paces, stopped at a red chair, pushed it back, twisted his body and dropped in the chair. He then moved his arm forward so that his hand touched the menu, grasped the menu and raised it towards him, and started reading. . . .

We know what it is like to have a meal in a restaurant; all this detail is unnecessary. If you have been to restaurants on a number of occasions, you will have acquired a schema or script containing general knowledge about likely kinds of events. Similarly:

> We need not ask why somebody wants to see our ticket when we enter a theater, or why one should be quiet, or how long it is appropriate to sit in one's seat. . . . Consider how difficult it would be to interpret 'second aisle on your right' without the detailed knowledge about theaters that the patron and usher both have. (Schank & Abelson, 1977, p. 37)

Providing Contexts for New Information

Scripts that form part of our knowledge can provide frames of reference to help us understand and remember events we experience. An event we cannot connect to something already known may be difficult to comprehend and retain. Sometimes we can help a person understand new information by providing a cue that specifies how it relates to what is already known. Read the passage below:

> The view was breathtaking. From the window one could see the crowd below. Everything looked extremely small from such a distance, but the colorful costumes could still be seen. Everyone seemed to be moving in one direction in an orderly fashion and there seemed to be little children as well as adults. The landing was gentle and luckily the atmosphere was such that no special suits had to be worn. At first there was a great deal of activity. Later, when the speeches started, the crowd quieted down. The man with the television camera took many shots of the setting and the crowd. Everyone was very friendly and seemed glad when the music started. (Bransford & Johnson, 1973, p. 412)

Most people who read this passage and are then asked to recall it can do so fairly accurately. But the sentence about the landing is rarely recalled, because it does not seem to fit into the structure of the passage. In a study by Bransford and Johnson (1973) some people simply read the passage, just as you have done. Others read the same passage, but it had an entirely different title: "A Space Trip to an Inhabited Planet." The people given this title, unlike the others, had no difficulty at all in recalling the sentence about the landing. The second title directed them toward that part of their existing knowledge that provided an adequate context, or frame of reference, for this particular information.

Sometimes a picture provides more effective context than words. In one study, students read the following passage:

> If the balloons popped the sound wouldn't be able to carry since everything would be too far away from the correct floor. A closed window would also prevent the sound from carrying, since most buildings tend to be well insulated. Since the whole operation depends on a steady flow of electricity, a break in the middle of the wire would also cause problems. Of course, the fellow could shout, but the human voice is not loud enough to carry that far. An additional problem is that a string could break on the instrument. Then there could be no accompaniment to the message. It is clear that the best situation would involve less distance. Then there would be fewer potential problems. With face-to-face contact, the least number of things could go wrong (Bransford & Johnson, 1972, p. 719)

Most people reading this passage on its own find it rather difficult to remember. However, some of the participants in another study by Bransford and Johnson (1972) had previously been shown the picture in Figure 7.1. (on page 93). These individuals recalled twice as much of the contents, on average, as people who had not seen the picture. In this instance, the picture served to direct the participants toward that area of their existing knowledge providing a meaningful context for the new information.

Is it especially easy to remember information when we have a

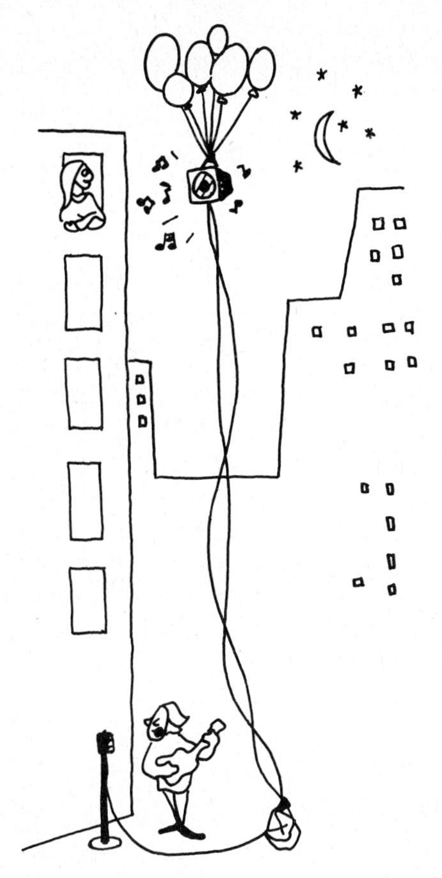

Figure 7.1 Picture context for balloon passage. *Source:* Bransford and Johnson (1972).

structured script? To answer this question, some students were asked to read one of two prose passages (Anderson, Spiro, & Anderson, 1978). One was a short story about dining in a fancy restaurant.

Most people have a clear script or schema with knowledge about the usual sequence of events involved in a restaurant meal. Typically, people make a reservation, arrive at the restaurant, sit at a table and receive menus, order food, and so on.

The other passage described a supermarket trip. The objects and actions in the story are familiar to those in the restaurant narrative, and the information in the supermarket passage is equally easy to understand. However, people do not have schemas or scripts for the detailed sequence of events in a supermarket visit, since activities are more variable and less tightly constrained than restaurant visits. For instance, the choice of items and the order in which they are collected in a supermarket is less constrained than the order of courses served in a meal.

A number of the objects and events described were identical in the two passages. The authors wanted to know if those items would be more frequently recalled if they had appeared in the more structured restaurant description. The findings confirmed this expectation and suggested that having a structured script does help people remember detailed information.

REPRESENTATION OF KNOWLEDGE IN MEMORY

The studies I have been describing demonstrate that people use their existing knowledge to help them comprehend and remember newly perceived information and events. But precisely how is meaningful knowledge represented in memory? Psychologists would like to be able to answer this difficult question. Two examples will illustrate some of the progress being made, and some of the difficulties encountered.

One approach is concerned with the manner of informational organization about items and their properties in a person's semantic memory (Collins & Quillian, 1969). They measured how long it took people to say certain propositions were true or false. Collins and Quillian thought that the time (*reaction time*) people took to make such decisions might tell us something about the knowledge organization used to arrive at a decision. For example, if we can decide much more quickly about the truth of the statement "A canary is yellow" than about "A canary breathes," this might suggest that there is a shorter or more direct link in semantic memory between representations of "a canary" and its attribute of "yellowness" than between "canary" and "breathing." Collins and Quillian

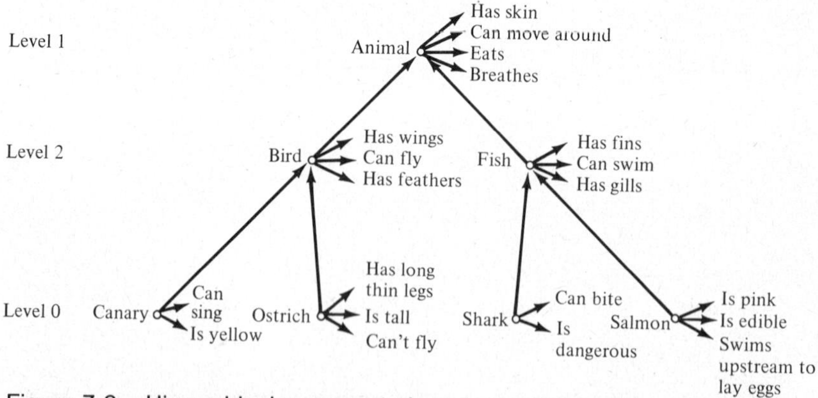

Figure 7.2 Hierarchical representation of semantic memory. *Source:* Collins and Quillian (1969).

proposed that semantic memory for the information contained in statements about items and their properties and attributes is hierarchically organized. Figure 7.2 shows one possible way such organization might be achieved. The diagram in the figure is essentially a theory, suggesting how knowledge might be represented in a person's memory.

It is assumed that statements presented at the same level or adjacent levels in the structure will be more quickly verified (or negated) than items at different levels. We can get some idea of Figure 7.2's accuracy by ascertaining if people's reaction times while they decide on the truth or falsity of various propositions are related to the distance between them in the figure. Examples of propositions are:

A canary has gills.
An ostrich can move around.
Salmon is edible.
A shark has wings.
A fish can swim.

According to Figure 7.2, deciding the truth about some of these sentences will necessitate more processing than deciding about others. If Figure 7.2 does describe how this knowledge is actually structured in human memory, it will be easier to establish that, for instance, "A canary is yellow" than "A canary has skin." Verifying the latter proposition involves retrieving information from different levels and transferring data between them. Verifying the former does not.

Collins and Quillian suggested that the time required to verify a statement will be directly related to the number of levels involved. If it was necessary to compare word entry with a property (for example, "A canary can fly"), it was posited that the reaction time would be longer by a constant amount than that of a judgement involving the same number of levels, but not involving matching an item with a property (for example, "A canary is a canary").

The first results Collins and Quillian obtained were broadly in line with what they expected. Average reaction times are shown in Figure 7.3. In general, the greater the number of levels involved, the higher the reaction time, as predicted, and having to compare a word entry with a property did add a roughly constant amount of time. Thus the findings shown in Figure 7.3 do appear to confirm the validity of the description of memory structure depicted in Figure 7.2.

However, there are a number of problems. One possibility is that the observed differences in reaction times might be due to other factors than the number of levels involved. Perhaps, for example, the words that are depicted on the same level in Figure 7.2 are ones that just happen to be closely associated to each other. Other difficulties were raised by fur-

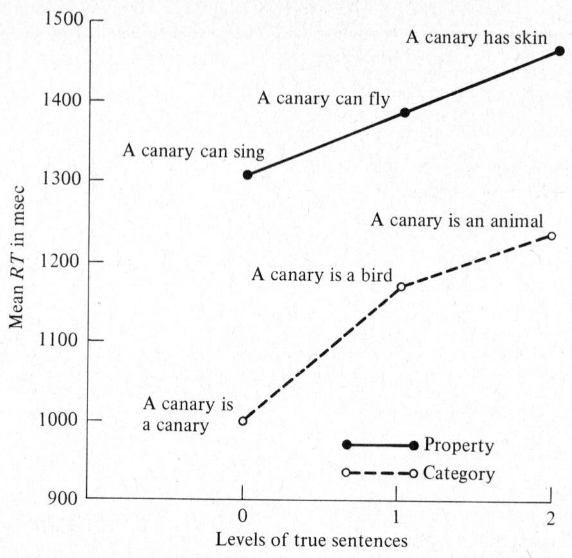

Figure 7.3 Semantic search times. *Source:* Collins and Quillian (1972).

ther experimental findings. For instance, the pattern of results shown in Figure 7.3 is not repeated if the sentences are presented in a different form. Carol Conrad (1972) presented sentences such as:

An animal has skin.
A bird has skin.
A canary has skin.

If Figure 7.2 correctly describes how these properties are represented in memory, the reaction times for verifying these statements should be equivalent to those for deciding about the kinds of statements used by Collins and Quillian, where the subject of the sentence was retained but the predicate statement varied, as in:

A canary is yellow.
A canary can fly.
A canary has skin.

However, Conrad's results were quite different. When she varied the subjects of her sentences (an animal, a bird, a canary) but retained a constant predicate statement (has skin), Conrad did not observe a consistent increase in reaction times as the number of levels increased. Furthermore, a study by Rips, Shoben, and Smith (1973) showed that questions involving adjacent items of information in a semantic hierarchy (for example, "Is a cantaloupe a melon?") are by no means always more quickly answered than questions involving information at different levels in the hierarchy (for example, "Is a cantaloupe a fruit?").

These results, and those of a number of other studies, have established that the straightforward hierarchical representation of information depicted in Figure 7.2 is almost certainly too simple to describe the actual organization of human knowledge. Nevertheless, by setting up a testable schematization of how knowledge *might* be structured, Collins and Quillian made a useful starting point for investigating the representation of knowledge in human memory.

Research into this problem continues. (For readable descriptions, see, for example, Norman & Rumelhart, 1975; Kintsch, 1977; Smith, 1978.) However, as Anderson (1976) points out, although it is not too difficult to set up plausible models depicting how knowledge *might* be arranged in memory, it is extremely difficult to determine how memory actually *is* organized in the human brain.

Finally, we shall consider an alternative approach to the investigation of the memory representation of meaningful descriptions. Walter Kintsch (1977) has been interested in the knowledge presented in prose passages. After reading such a passage, we do not retain the exact form of words. Kintsch points out that the meaning in a textual passage can be represented by a number of linked *propositions.* Consider, for example, the following extract:

Turbulence forms at the edge of a wing and grows in strength over its surface, contributing to the lift of a supersonic aircraft.

The meaningful content of this sentence can be depicted as a number of propositions, shown in Figure 7.4.

The figure shows how a number of different propositions are related to each other. For example, Proposition 1, concerning the formation of turbulence, is directly linked to Proposition 2, the location at which it forms, to Proposition 4, concerning the growth of such turbu-

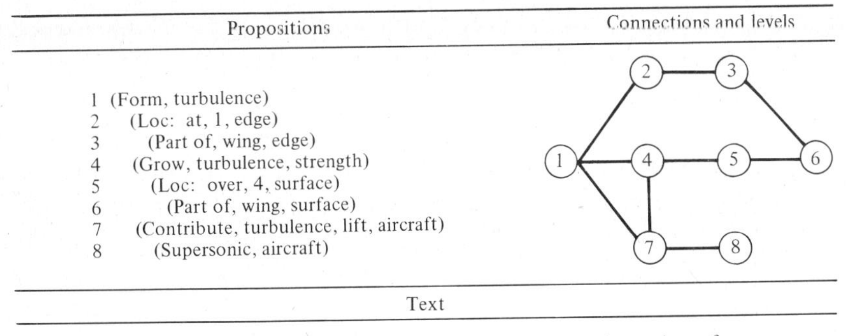

Figure 7.4 Propositions contained in text presented by Kintsch (1976).

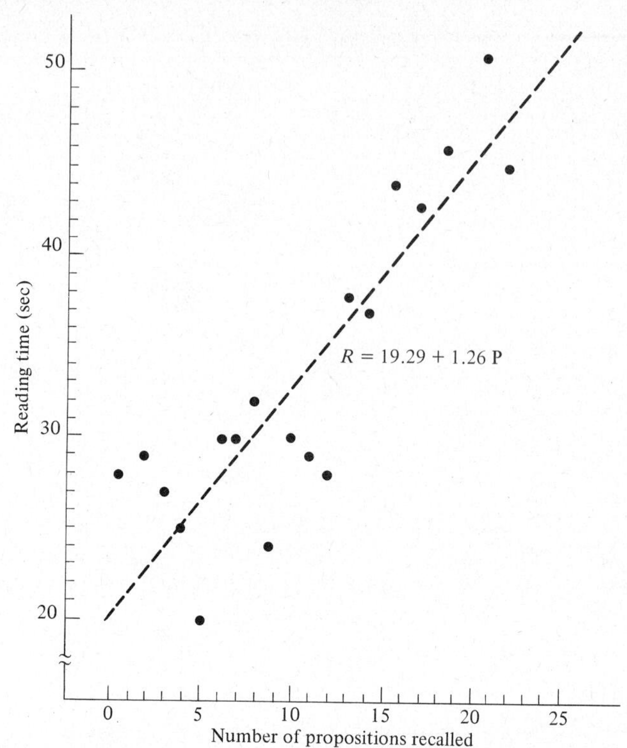

Figure 7.5 Reading time as a function of the number of propositions recalled. *Source:* Kintsch (1976).

lence, and to Proposition 7, the contribution of turbulence to the lift of the aircraft.

One way to test the validity of this way of representing meaningful knowledge is to measure the accuracy of the predictions it generates. Kintsch's model has been used to predict the difficulty of different passages. It is reasonable to suppose that the amount of new information a passage contains will be a factor contributing to the difficulty of that passage for a particular student. Kintsch suggests that propositions are formed according to rules known to a reader. If a sentence contains a number of propositions, the reader should be able to derive a list of the propositions contained in it, and the reader's list of propositions will correspond to the information possessed by the writer of the passage. The amount of processing the reader must undertake to comprehend the passage will be directly related to the number of propositions.

If the number of propositions in a passage gives an indication of the amount of material to be acquired and remembered, measures of the number of propositions should predict human performance more accurately than measures of superficial qualities of a passage, such as the number of words. Furthermore, if the amount of mental processing required to perform a task is related to the number of propositions, as Kintsch suggests, then the greater the number of propositions (assuming the length of the passage is constant), the more time will be necessary to understand the passage. Kintsch tested this prediction in a simple experiment. As he expected, he found that with a constant number of words, the greater the number of propositions in a passage, the longer the time people needed to read it. When Kintsch tested people's recall of a passage containing 25 propositions and consisting of 70 words total, he found a clear linear relationship between recall of the propositions and the length of time spent in studying the passage (Figure 7.5). That is, the more time spent in reading, the greater the number of propositions recalled.

Chapter 8
Memory Development in Children

Adults and older children remember most things better than young children. Why is this so?

There was a notable increase of research activities on children's memory development during the 1970s. The research findings in this field were unexpected and exciting, and had both practical applicability and implications for broad understanding of the nature of human development. One outcome of research into the development of memory was a demonstration that not all aspects of memory improve as we get older, as was noted in Chapter 1. Also, while older children do outperform younger individuals at many tasks of remembering, some of the skills enabling older people to remember more than young children are ones that can be learned fairly quickly and easily. These skills do not need a lengthy period of time to develop.

We also noted in Chapter 1 that memory is not entirely separate from other functions of human cognition, and that the ability to remember is crucially important in a wide range of situations. It may be possible to raise young children's memory skills toward the levels customarily observed in older children. If this can be achieved, we could expect widespread gains in abilities contributing toward a child's education and other spheres of life where competence depends upon learning and remembering.

EXPLAINING AGE-RELATED IMPROVEMENTS

If I ask you to say why a 15-year-old boy outperforms a 5-year-old at a task demanding learning, thinking, or remembering, it is quite likely that you will reply, "Because he's older," as if the concept of development provided an explanation of age-related changes. But, of course, it does not. To say that development, as such, actually *causes* an improvement is like saying that improvements are caused by the passing of time (Belmont, 1978). Time does not actually change anything: It merely provides opportunities for events to occur. Certainly, many human attributes are related to age; the older someone is, the greater the amount of time that has elapsed in which events causing change can occur. For the older child, more time has elapsed during which skills can be learned or knowledge acquired.

If the probability of a person gaining a particular skill in any 1-year period is 1 in 10, irrespective of age, the likelihood of a 15-year-old having acquired that skill will be much higher (by a factor of 3) than the probability of a 5-year-old having gained it. And if we subsequently draw a graph showing how the proportion of children possessing that skill is related to children's ages, the graph will show the steady progression found with many age-related human characteristics (Figure 8.1a). However, it would be wrong to conclude from the steadily rising line that we are looking at the gradual "development" of the skill. The curve showing average performance by a group of children may not be at all representative of what happens in each individual child. Conceivably, the skill may take only 5 minutes to acquire: In that case, the curve on the imagi-

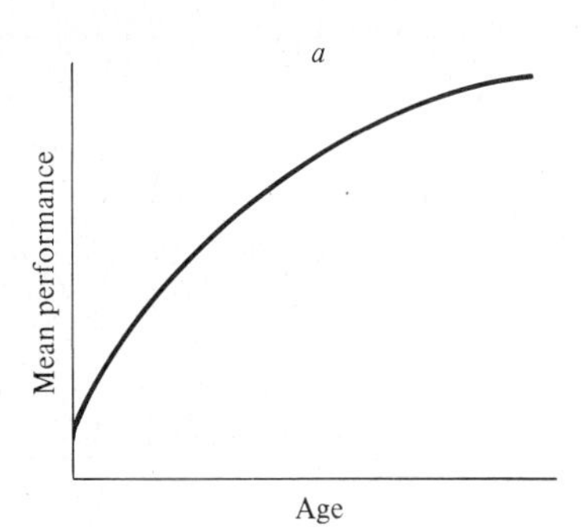

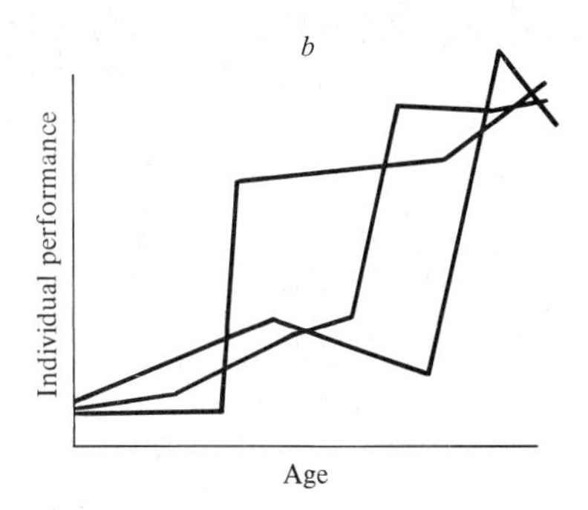

Figure 8.1 Age and performance. (a.) hypothetical curve showing averaged data; (b.) some of the contributing individual performance curves for particular children.

nary graph for an individual would take the form of a horizontal line depicting a low level of performance, followed by a near vertical line indicating rapid learning, and then followed by a further horizontal line showing a higher level of performance (Figure 8.1b). In this case, the sole reason for the better average performance of older children (Figure 8.1a), lies in the fact that the number of opportunities for learning the skill is related to the amount of time one has lived.

The habit of regarding time as a cause of change is a deeply engrained one, as John Belmont observes:

> Laymen and professionals alike speak and write as though age *causes* differences among people. Thus, we might easily say 'She reads better than he, but then again she's older,' and we are not put off by the development research title, 'The effects of age upon memory span for nonsense syllables,' even though age is nothing but the ticking of a clock, and certainly never increased a child's memory for nonsense syllables or anything else. (Belmont, 1978, p. 156)

Belmont also points out that the apparently steady and gradual increase in recall accuracy as children get older (as is apparently demonstrated by performance curves like the one in Figure 8.1a) is quite illusory as an indication of what actually happens in individual children. He reports observing, on one occasion, that recall accuracy in a group of 80 children, aged 10 to 17 years, increased linearly and reliably with age. However, closer inspection of their individual scores revealed that age only accounted for about a quarter of the variability between individuals in recall accuracy. This indicates that "the really important performance differences were not even related to, much less explained by, anything so simple as gross maturation." (Belmont, 1978, p. 154.) In fact, there is considerable variation in the age at which most intellectual abilities are gained.

The essential point is that older children recall things more accurately than younger children not simply "because they have developed" but because they have managed to acquire skills that the young children lack. For a number of reasons, some abilities cannot be acquired early in life. However, a number of the skills underlying the better memory task performance of older people compared with young children are ones that can be acquired at a younger age than they customarily are.

DEVELOPMENTAL CHANGES IN REMEMBERING

Before examining the detailed reasons for memory improvement in older children, I will give a brief overview in the form of a summary that sketches the broad changes producing age-related increases in recall accuracy.

As children get older, they become more mentally active, more knowledgeable, and more resourceful in making use of the mental processing capacities for performing various cognitive tasks, including remembering. The older person is better equipped with plans and strategies for organizing and controlling his own mental processes in a manner effective for meeting the demands of memory tasks. An older person also possesses more knowledge that can be used to facilitate processing and organization of new events to be remembered. Older people, in addition, are better at assessing the requirements of a situation when remembering is necessary. They are more likely to have acquired plans and strategies useful for performing memory tasks and they are better at choosing appropriate strategies, at devising new routines, plans, and strategies when existing ones are inadequate, inefficient, or nonexistent.

In short, to return to the garden plot metaphor introduced in Chapter 1, the older person, compared with younger children, is a more effective cultivator of the processing capacities remembering depends upon. Or, to use a computer metaphor, the computing processes of older individuals are accompanied by both better programs for coordinating the necessary processes and more self-programming skills for improving remembering—by constructing new routines and modifying existing ones.

We can now return to the evidence concerning the causes of human memory development. The possible causes of age-related memory increases can be considered under four broad categories. These are:

1. structural changes in basic memory capacities
2. activities and strategies
3. knowledge
4. metamemory.

The above groupings are not mutually exclusive, and it is sometimes difficult to decide which of the four categories a particular influence fits best. However, it is useful and convenient to categorize the diverse factors found to contribute to age-related improvements in remembering (see Brown, 1975 and Flavell, 1977 for good reviews). I shall mention some, but not all, of the causes of improving memory.

I shall not consider the development of memory during the first two years of a child's life. Undoubtedly these are crucial years, although we do not have as clear an understanding of the memory changes taking place during this period as we do for the subsequent years of childhood.

DO STRUCTURAL CHANGES OCCUR?

There is ample evidence that factors falling within each of the other three categories listed above make substantial contributions to memory development. In the case of structural changes, however, the situation is strikingly different.

For a long time it was assumed that a child's developing ability to remember depended upon capacity changes taking place in the basic physiological structure of the memory system. But there is virtually no strong evidence to support this belief. There is abundant evidence that as children get older they do become better at remembering. However, the view that this improvement is due to the memory system becoming bigger or better in a way closely linked to maturation of the underlying physiological structures does not receive any firm support.

Physiological maturation might lead to basic memory capacity improvements in a number of ways. One suggestion is that the number of places or *slots* (Chi, 1976) available for short-term retention of items might increase. Another is that memory traces might fade at a rate that decreases with age. Chi (1976) and Huttenlocher and Burke (1976) examined the available evidence, and they concluded that no firm evidence exists for either of these suggestions. It is always harder to prove that a particular factor *does not* exert an influence than it is to show that a factor *does* have an effect.

Several kinds of information indicate that structural changes do not make a big contribution to memory development (except, perhaps, in the initial two years of life). First, as I demonstrated in Chapter 1, young children perform just as well at a number of memory tasks as adults. Therefore, if structural changes do nevertheless contribute to age-related improvements, the changes must be ones that influence performance at some memory tasks but not at others. This is not impossible, but it seems unlikely. The second kind of evidence against any structural change theory lies in the fact that the alternative, nonstructural, categories of change appear to be able to account quite adequately for the observed changes in remembering. It thus appears that no unexplained changes remain to be accounted for by an explanation based on structural changes.

A third type of evidence comes from studies investigating children's performance when they are given a variety of different memory tests. If basic memory capacity is the major influence upon how well subjects remember things, we would expect to find an individual achieving similar levels of success on a variety of different memory tasks. Over a range of tests, some people would reliably perform well; others, with poor memories, would do badly. However, the facts suggest otherwise. In one investigation, 5-year-olds were each given 11 different memory tasks (Stevenson, Parker, & Wilkinson, 1975). When the authors computed the correlations between each child's scores on all the tests, they found average correlations to be very low (+.14). Correlations of this order are far too small to serve as a basis for predicting how well a child will do in a memory test. The absence of closer relationships between an individual's scores on the different tests provides a further indication that differences in basic memory capacity do not have a great influence on remembering or on the development of memory.

It would be premature to rule out the possibility that changes in the basic anatomical and physiological hardware of memory systems continue to take place throughout the years of early childhood, and make a contribution to improved remembering. However, in the absence of definite evidence for this view, the practical option is to concentrate on examining those factors that clearly do influence remembering—namely activities, strategies, knowledge, and metamemory.

ACTIVITIES AND STRATEGIES

As children get older, they respond in increasingly active ways to situations requiring recall. Older children are more likely to do various things that help them remember. Some activities aiding memory are automatic, and others are deliberately undertaken. Some activities are performed consciously and others occur without awareness. In this section the main concern will be with actions that can be both conscious and deliberate. The terms strategy and plan are often applied to the more complex of these activities.

An intelligent adult calls upon a variety of strategies to help remembering. These include labeling, elaborating, using mediators to connect separate items or relate them to each other, organizing materials in various ways, rehearsing, and other planned activities. As we discovered in Chapter 4, activities like these lead to increased remembering in children and adults. It seems likely that older children will have acquired a larger repertoire of strategies than younger children, and will be more adept at making use of them.

Rehearsal

Rehearsal activities can substantially increase remembering. We learned in Chapter 4 that differences in item rehearsal partly accounted for the shape of the serial position curve, and for the frequent finding that items occurring early in a list become more highly consolidated than items presented later. When children younger than 5 years are asked to remember things, they do not rehearse spontaneously. This is hardly surprising: Until a child goes to school, the skills underlying deliberate recall are unlikely to have been fully taught or much practiced. The task of remembering for its own sake is not a familiar one for many preschool children.

The poor performance at memory tasks of those children who do not rehearse leads us to ask two questions. First, is the young children's poor remembering caused by their not rehearsing? Secondly, if those young children who do not spontaneously rehearse can be induced to do so, will their remembering immediately improve, or might they be simply too young to benefit from rehearsal? Researchers use the term *mediation deficiency* to denote the latter possibility, and *production deficiency* for the former (Brown, 1975).

In order to investigate the possible contributions of rehearsal to children's memory, we need to observe rehearsal activity. It is always possible to ask a person if she is rehearsing, of course, but subjective reports are often unreliable, especially in young children. A more direct measure of rehearsal would be preferable. Fortunately, young children (but not adults) are prone to move their lips when they rehearse. The observing experimenter is thereby provided with a useful indication of the amount of rehearsal a child undertakes. In one study (Flavell, Beach, & Chinsky, 1966) lip movements were observed as children looked at some common objects that they were told to remember. Seventeen out of 20 10-year-olds were seen to move their lips, but only 2 out of 20 5-year-olds did so. Furthermore, at each age the children moving their lips recalled a larger number of items than the children who did not. These findings are definitely consistent with the view that rehearsing makes a positive contribution to memory.

To discover if instructing the nonrehearsers to rehearse would lead them to remember more, Keeney, Cannizzo, and Flavell (1967) gave careful instructions to children aged 6 and 7 years who did not rehearse spontaneously. They were told to whisper the names of pictured objects they had been shown, until the moment they were told to start recalling. The children had no trouble in following these instructions. When they did so, recall performance improved substantially—it equaled that of those children who rehearsed spontaneously.

Clearly, rehearsing does lead to improved remembering. The findings show that 6- and 7-year-olds who do not normally rehearse are capable of doing so when simple instructions are given, and that they remember things better when they do rehearse. Since the children are capable of acquiring a rehearsal strategy so easily, it might seem surprising that they have not discovered it for themselves. One possibility is that they simply have not gained the *habit* of regularly applying the strategy, although they are competent to do so. A child may find it more difficult to adopt a relatively unfamiliar strategy than to behave in a passive manner, especially when the memory task is itself unfamiliar. Faced with new and unfamiliar tasks, many people are prone to rely on familiar and habitual solutions, even when different activities would be more effective. Children are equally drawn to what is habitual and familiar to them. John Holt pointed out, in a book called *How Children Fail* (1964), that when children confront tasks of classroom learning they all too frequently revert to activities that are more immature and less strategic than ones they have recently learned, especially when they are anxious or afraid.

Other Strategic Activities

Like rehearsal, the various other activities and strategies that can contribute to input processing (Chapter 4) are used increasingly as children get older. Adults and older children are more likely than younger children to group and organize materials, to form mediating links, and to use visual imagery effectively. As I demonstrated in Chapter 1, older children are also better at undertaking effective strategic activities when they try retrieving materials stored in memory. This leads to increased recall in some circumstances, but not in others. When 6-year-olds were given cues carefully directing their retrieval activities, obviating the need for a deliberate strategy, they recalled roughly as many items (about 20 words out of 24) as 12-year-olds. But when the cues were either less specific or absent altogether, the younger children recalled only around 10 items, whereas the 12-year-olds remembered 16 words, on average. The experimenter (Kobigasigawa, 1974) had established that all the items were familiar to the youngest children, but it was found that the older subjects more frequently used a category search strategy for retrieving items. When category cues were provided, younger children would typically recall one item only, and then proceed to the next cue. Older children who received a cue word were more likely to use it as the basis for a careful search for all the items in the appropriate category.

The findings of a large number of experimental investigations confirm that adults and older children are more planning-oriented and strategic than young children in situations involving remembered information. In general, the greater the extent that performance can be influenced by people adopting a deliberate plan or strategy, the larger the development differences that are found when children of different ages are compared.

An effective strategy may include a number of components. Combining rehearsal and organizing activities can be highly effective, for instance. As we have seen, simple rehearsal improves remembering, and so does categorizing or grouping the materials one needs to remember.

Age-related differences in organizing perceived events have been observed in a number of memory tasks. Thus Moely (1969) found that when older children were told to remember pictures of various objects, they typically reordered the individual items, arranging them into categories, but young children did not. This could be changed by means similar to rehearsal instructions. When young children were carefully shown how to group the pictures into categories, and were encouraged to do so, their recall scores improved.

A good strategy may include a number of components. As we have seen, straightforward rehearsal improves remembering, and so too does grouping or categorizing the materials one needs to remember. A combination of rehearsal and organizational activities, for example, can be especially effective.

Both rehearsal and organizing activities may be achieved with varying degrees of effectiveness. They are not "all or nothing" acts: The success of either depends upon the particular steps that are followed. For instance, children's rehearsing is more effective if they repeat the names of successive objects in a cumulative manner, repeatedly rehearsing the complete sequence up to the most recent item, than if they simply rehearse one item at a time, as it is presented (Kingsley & Hagen, 1969). A child needs to learn how to rehearse materials in a manner suited to the particular features of each occasion where rehearsing is appropriate. Children have to become able to time their rehearsals properly, taking advantage of the intervals between successive items or events (Hagen & Stanovick, 1977). They must learn to rehearse cumulatively (Ornstein, Naus, & Liberty, 1975). Not until some time after children are old enough to profit from activities such as rehearsing and organizing do they gain the habit of using them spontaneously, and the ability to adapt them to the varied demands of different memory tasks.

It was suggested in Chapter 4 that strategies are helpful because they extend the input processing items receive. We can regard differences in mental processing (which we cannot actually observe) as having a direct effect on remembering, while strategies (which we can both observe and control) have a less direct influence. Their influence is exerted through their effect on processing. It is likely that differences in the extensiveness of the perceptual processing that takes place at input are a major cause of developmental differences in memory. If that is the case, procedures to ensure that children of different ages perform equivalent processing upon new information should have the effect of minimizing age differences in remembering.

In order to find out if this happens, Geis and Hall (1976) tested children using a procedure similar to that of the adult studies by Tulving and Watkins (1975), described in Chapter 3. Presentation of single words was preceded by orienting questions, designed to make subjects analyze the superficial attributes (for example, "Is the word printed in uppercase letters?") or the phonemic features (for example, "Is it a flower?"). Later, when the children tried to remember the words, it was found that recall was closely related to the kind of input analysis required by the questions, a result replicating the findings of the research by Tulving and Watkins on adult subjects.

More importantly, there were no differences in recall between older and younger children performing the same level of input analysis. The fact that age differences were eliminated in this study clearly supports the view that developmental improvements in remembering are caused, at least in part, by differences in the perceptual analysis occurring at the input of new materials. When highly elaborate semantic processing is necessary, however, some age differences in recall are observed. For these observations, see Geis and Hall, 1978; Ghatala, Carbonari, and Bobele, 1980.

USING EXISTING KNOWLEDGE

The processing taking place as an event is perceived will partly depend upon the perceiver's existing knowledge concerning the new input. Imagine that you are walking in a field, and you see a cow. How might this input be analyzed? Most adults have a fair amount of knowledge about cows. They know, for instance:

Cows are animals.
Cows have four legs.
Cows are mammals.
Cows produce milk.
Cows are domesticated.
Cows live on farms.

When you see a cow you may have access to any of these items of knowledge. The description you retain in memory after seeing the cow will be influenced by the knowledge you possess about cows and their attributes. (In more general terms, if a perceived item has meaning to a person, it is because the input can be related to something already known.) If the description you store in memory after seeing the cow is connected to any of the above pieces of information about cows' attributes, the same information may serve as an effective retrieval cue for helping you to remember that it was a cow you saw. If you next see a horse, it is immediately recognized as being different.

Imagine now that the same cow is standing in the identical field, but on this occasion perceived not by yourself but by a Martian (with a human brain!) who has just landed on earth. This is the first animal he has seen. Our Martian friend does not know anything about cows, and therefore his input analysis is highly restricted. The resulting description stored in memory is correspondingly restricted, perhaps limited to physical dimensions. A less extreme instance would be one where I see an unfamiliar rare plant today, and tomorrow I am shown a plant of similar size and color, and asked whether it belongs to the same species. Because my knowledge of plants is very limited, my input processing would be minimal. Therefore, the resulting memory description would be highly restricted.

Consequently, I could not decide if tomorrow's plant is the same species as today's. A botanist, however, would know more than I do about plant life, and would find it much easier to recognize a particular plant. When the botanist perceived the plant, he or she would be able to draw upon a much more extensive knowledge about plant attributes, leading to a more detailed (elaborate) description being retained. And, in consequence, he would have considerably greater recognition accuracy.

Making Inferences

As children grow, so does their knowledge about the world. Knowledge affects an individual's retrieval strategies as well as influencing perceptual analysis of events. It determines the kinds of inferences and reconstructive processes that can occur when the child tries to remember (see Chapter 7). As children get older, they rely increasingly on making inferences when trying to recall information. In an investigation by Brown, Smiley, Day, Townsend, and Lawton (1977), children tried to recall a story they had heard. When the investigators examined attempted recall, they paid close attention to incorrect items (*intrusions*) in the children's recall attempts. (Incorrect items are those absent from the correct story.) It was found that the proportion of intrusions relevant to the story increased from 51% in children aged 7 to 79% in 13-year-olds.

In order to gain a more direct indication of the extent to which children infer information not explicitly provided, Paris and Lindauer (1976) presented sentences like:

> "Her friend swept the kitchen floor."
> "Her friend swept the kitchen floor with a broom."

Subsequently the word *broom* was used as a recall cue ("What sentence does *broom* remind you of?"). The authors reasoned that if children who received the first of the two sentences inferred that a broom was used, the cue would be effective. If they did not make such an inference, presenting the cue word would not help them. However, all children receiving the second sentence should be helped by the recall cue, because its value for them does not depend upon a child having made an inference.

The findings of this study provide further evidence that older children are more likely to make inferences. The cue helped 11-year-olds whether or not the word had appeared in the original sentence. Clearly, the 11-year-olds were inferring the presence of a broom. However, the recall cue was ineffective for 7-year-olds if the original sentence had not made explicit mention of the broom. In this condition, only about 20% of the sentences were recalled. When the original sentence *had* mentioned a broom, the cue produced correct recall in 70% of occasions.

Very similar findings were obtained when the recall cue referred to the *consequences* of something stated in the original sentence rather than to the instrument (that is, *broom*) with which an action was performed.

To help us understand the effects of knowledge upon remembering, it is useful to consider one situation in which the amount of knowledge is *not* related to age and the influence of knowledge is *not* confounded with other age-related factors that affect remembering. One approach has been to examine memory for chess positions in children and adults. It is possible to compare remembering children who have considerable chess knowledge with adults who know less about the game. Chi (1978) tested 6 children, averaging 10 years of age, who were all good chess players. She formed a comparison group of adult subjects who could play chess but were not advanced players. The degree of chess knowledge was assessed by measuring the speed and appropriateness of moves, and it was established that the children were faster at solving a chess problem (the Knights' Tour) and made a higher proportion of correct moves.

The participants in Chi's experiment were shown a chess position for 10 seconds. Immediately afterward, they tried to place the appropriate pieces in the correct positions on a blank chessboard. Chi found that children's immediate recall (9.3 pieces recalled in the correct position, on average) was considerably better than that of adults (5.9 pieces). This contrasted with the pattern of results from a test of memory for digit lists. As Figure 8.2 shows, children's immediate recall, compared with adults, was superior for chess positions but inferior for digits.

The child subjects' superior knowledge of chess gave them a clear advantage in the particular memory task concerning that knowledge. However, in the tests of memory for digits the children did *not* possess knowledge the adults lacked, and the older participants remembered more items.

We have discussed knowledge and strategies as separate influences upon remembering. In reality, just as rehearsal and organization may operate in combination, a person's strategies and knowledge may act jointly to improve remembering. For example, the way a child groups items or imposes organization upon them depends upon what he knows about them. The experiment by Ceci and Howe (1978b) described in Chapter 6 demonstrated that flexible retrieval strategies can increase recall: It illustrates a situation where the ability to perform a strategic activity (switching between different ways of grouping the items) depends upon another activity (organizing pictures into thematic and semantic categories) and upon having appropriate knowledge (about the items).

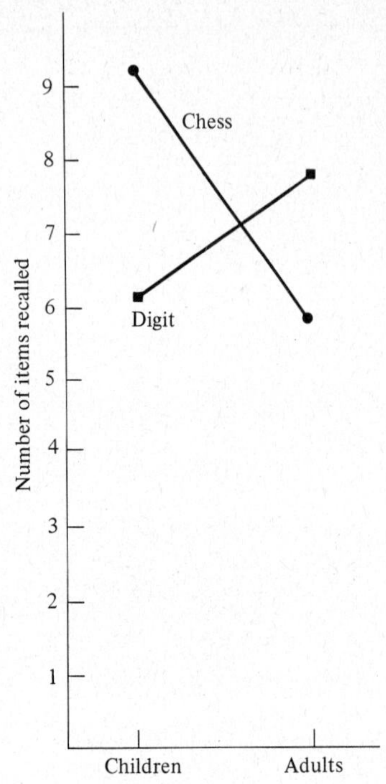

Figure 8.2 Immediate recall of digits and chess positions by children and adults. *Source:* Chi (1978).

METAMEMORY

Adults, as we have seen, do numerous things to help themselves remember. They have the advantage of knowing more about whatever is to be remembered, and being able to call upon various strategies. In addition, they are more aware than young children about how to remember information and events.

The term *metamemory* refers to awareness and general knowledge about one's own memory processes (Flavell, 1977). This can take various forms; for example, simply being aware that an item needs to be remembered; knowing one's own abilities and limitations; knowing how the characteristics of a task influence its difficulty; knowing when a strategic activity will improve remembering, and which one to use; and knowing how to adapt strategies to unfamiliar tasks. Any college student will have acquired a repertoire of knowledge on how to remember, but the young child lacks this repertoire.

Most adult learners possess a multitude of good strategies and are able to choose one suitable for a particular task. In general, the ability to remember things does not depend so much upon a person possessing any one particular strategy as upon an ability to select and modify appropriate plans and strategies; one "finds the right tool for the job" when something must be remembered. In other words:

> Different strategies are effective in different situations, and the mature memorizer is able to evaluate the task demands accurately enough to come up with an appropriate choice. (Campione & Brown, 1977, p. 374)

As children get older, they become better at knowing what to do whenever remembering is needed. Their power to control and execute the necessary activities increases. Metamemory processes vary in complexity and sophistication, and a very young child cannot even distinguish between simply seeing an event and attending to it. By the age of 3, however, most children know that requests to remember something demand some kind of response. In an experiment (Wellman, Ritter, & Flavell, 1975), 3-year-olds watched the investigator hide a toy under one of a number of identical cups. Then the children were told to *wait* with the toy or to *remember* where the toy was hidden. Those children who were told to remember did behave differently; for instance, they were more likely to touch the item or look at it. Furthermore, 3-year-olds who had been forewarned that they would be asked to recall an event remembered it more accurately than children given no advance warning.

But young children have only a limited awareness of what they can do to remember things. Appel, Cooper, McCarrell, Sims-Knight, Yussen, and Flavell (1972) found that 4-year-olds shown some items after being told to remember them acted no differently than after receiving instructions simply telling them to attend. And the different instructions did not affect the accuracy of 11-year-olds placed in the same situation—but when told to remember, they engaged in activities such as categorizing and rehearsing, and as a result recalled more.

The distinctions between simply seeing something and attending to it, and between attending to an event and remembering it, are clear and straightforward for older people, but they do have to be acquired.

Children also become more accurate at judging their own memory capacities with increasing age. They learn that various aspects of a memory task can influence the level of difficulty, and they learn how to select and use plans and strategies particularly appropriate for various kinds of tasks.

To compare older and younger children's accuracy at judging their own memory abilities and limitations, Flavell, Friedrichs, and Hoyt (1970) asked participants aged between 4 and 10 years to predict how well they would perform at a memory test presenting sequences of pictures. Among the youngest subjects, aged from 4 to 6 years, more than

54% made unrealistically optimistic predictions. They thought they would correctly recall the longest sequences, containing 10 items. The older children's predictions were considerably more accurate: Only a quarter of 7- and 10-year-olds unrealistically judged they would be able to remember the longest lists. Yussen and Levy (1975) found that young adults could predict memory span performance with considerably more accuracy than children.

The adults guessed that they would recall 5.9 items, on average, and their actual scores averaged 5.52. The difference between young children's estimated and actual recall was much greater. Four-year-olds' estimated recall averaged 8.2 items, compared with the actual score of 3.3, and in children aged 8 the respective estimated and actual scores were 6.6 and 4.7.

It might be argued that young children are simply poor at estimating *anything*, and in that case their poor memory predictions might indicate a general lack of judgement, rather than ignorance about memory as such. However, children are much better at predicting their performance at other skills—for example, estimating how far they can jump. The deficiency in predicting remembering seems to be a fairly specific one.

A number of investigators have examined children's knowledge about the effects of task variables upon remembering. Moynahan (1973) found that 10-year-old children were more likely than 7-year-olds to say that lists of items organized into categories would be easier to remember than lists of unrelated materials. Similarly, children aged 9 and older are more likely than 6-year-olds to predict that pairs of related words would be more easily recalled than pairs of words chosen at random (Kreutzer, Leonard, & Flavell, 1975).

Children become aware at an early age that it is easier to remember a small amount of material than a great amount. But only a minority of 4-year-olds realize that it is usually easier to recognize items than to recall them (Spear & Flavell, 1977). Just over 50% of 6-year-olds, but over 90% of children aged 8 and above, are sensitive to the fact that it is more difficult to keep something in memory for a longer than a shorter time. Kreutzer, Leonard, and Flavell (1975) asked children whether it would make any difference if, after being told a friend's telephone number, they dialed immediately or had a drink of water first. Another study was designed to discover if children who had been told they would have to remember something for a long time would act differently than they would after being told to remember for only a short period (Rogoff, Newcombe, & Kagan, 1974). Eight-year-olds looked at pictures for differing lengths of time, according to whether they were asked to remember them for 4 minutes, a day, or a week. But children aged 4 to 6 years spent the same amount of time inspecting the pictures, irrespective of how long they were told to remember them.

CONCLUSION

Experimental research gives us a fair understanding of why adults are better at remembering information and events than young children are. To a large extent the reasons older people are more successful lie in things they actually *do* to remember. As we have seen, when younger children who do not perform certain strategic activities spontaneously are carefully instructed to do so, as in the rehearsal studies, their recall often improves dramatically. Findings of this kind encourage us to be optimistic about the possibility of memory improvement, in older people as well as children, by appropriate instruction and training. Individuals can learn to engage in strategic activities that do produce good remembering. We saw in Chapter 1 that remembering is basic to a wide range of important human abilities. Therefore, we can expect instructions increasing people's memory skills to have widespread and powerful effects. In the following chapter I shall describe the findings of some studies investigating the effects of training and instruction in better recall.

Chapter 9
Improving Memory

INTRODUCTION: REMEMBERING CAN BE INCREASED

In this final chapter we will mention some of the things that have been done in order to help people remember. We have already encountered a number of factors that influence remembering, but they will not be surveyed again in any detail. After making a brief statement about the broad causes of improved remembering, ways to help mentally retarded people, who are often seriously handicapped by poor remembering, will be mentioned. Finally, drawing upon some of the evidence from earlier chapters, I shall summarize some of the practical steps that one can follow in order to improve remembering.

By this stage it will be clear that if you fail to remember something it is not simply because you have a "bad memory." Your success in remembering information and events depends to a large extent upon activities you are able to control.

A number of the causes of better memory have been introduced in previous chapters. A major factor is the processing taking place at the input of new events. The perceptual analysis occurring at this stage forms the description of the event, or memory trace, that is stored in memory. If the trace is subsequently located, an event may be remembered.

The input processing's extensiveness will depend in part upon the requirements of the situation. Processing can be experimentally manipulated by, for instance, asking different kinds of questions concerning items about to be perceived. It also depends upon what the individual already knows in relation to the new event. If the outcome of input processing is to form a stored description specifying its precise meaning, it is likely that the description will be distinctive in memory, and therefore easy to locate, as long as conditions at the time of recall are favorable for gaining memory trace access. If the input processing is less extensive, on the other hand, and the analysis has been insufficient to form a highly distinctive representation of the event, it is less likely that the memory trace will remain accessible for a long period of time. However, as we have seen, in certain instances memory traces are formed by restricted (nonsemantic) perceptual analysis at the input stage, and may remain highly distinctive.

A variety of strategies, plans, and activities are effective as ways to improve remembering, largely because they lead to the materials being extensively processed at the time of input. What a person actually remembers largely depends upon what he or she *does* with the to-be-remembered information, so it is often possible to increase remembering by instructing the person to engage in the most effective activities. Memory improvements have been demonstrated in numerous circumstances. For instance, the series of experiments by Craik and Tulving described in Chapter 3 showed that when people attend to the meaning of a briefly perceived word, they are much more likely to recall it later than if they have attended only to the form of the world. Also, engaging in any of a number of stategies that involve rehearsing, organizing, and mediating can increase remembering (Chapter 4); and so can effective strategies for retrieving items from memory (Chapter 6). Furthermore, when young children are instructed to undertake certain actions or strategies that are spontaneously performed by older people more proficient at memory tasks, the young children's performance typically rises toward that of the older subjects. In short, there is ample evidence that in many circumstances people remember things better if they undertake the activities more appropriate to the particular task.

If we *can* help people to remember better, there are many reasons why we ought to do so. Quite apart from the obvious desirability of improving memory, there is the fact that improved ability to retain information leads to better performance on a range of important human abilities (see Chapter 1). In many situations, differences between people's essential skills are caused largely by performance differences in the memory components involved. In addition, the sheer difficulty of many intellectual tasks depends largely upon the demands they make on memory.

Chapter 1 mentioned some of the human abilities in which remembering plays a crucial role. The list could be greatly extended: Memory is vital for numerous skills. At times its importance is not immediately clear. Consider, for instance, Kail's investigations of children's moral judgements (1979). The Swiss developmental psychologist Jean Piaget has shown that up to the age of around 7 years, children who are told about other children's misdemeanors and asked to judge the degree of guilt involved typically decide according to the consequence of the action, rather than the intentions. For example, a child who accidentally breaks 10 cups is judged to be naughtier than a child who deliberately breaks 1 cup. Piaget has claimed evidence like this reveals important developmental changes in children's moral reasoning.

It is possible, however, that the correct explanation of this finding has more to do with memory than with reasoning. Feldman, Klosson, Parsons, Rholes, and Ruble (1976) thought that the failure of young children to consider intentions when making moral judgements might have been due to their failure to *remember* the intentions, rather than to a failure in reasoning. They noticed that the children in Piaget's studies had been given fairly lengthy descriptions of the misdemeanors, and that the information referring to the child's intentions came at the beginning of the story. To test the suggestion that failure to take intentions into account might be due to the intentions having simply been forgotten, the investigators reversed Piaget's procedure. The outcome was described at the beginning of each story and the child's intention indicated at the end. In these circumstances, the children were better at recalling the end of a story than the beginning. When a child's intentions were described near the end of a description, the 5-year-olds, like older people, made moral judgements taking more account of the protagonist's intentions than of the outcome. In brief, the findings Piaget thought demonstrated a basic deficiency in young children's social reasoning were actually caused by age-related limitations in memory. It is very likely that memory limitations are a frequent cause of poor performance by young children at reasoning tasks.

HELPING RETARDED PEOPLE REMEMBER

A number of investigators have conducted studies demonstrating that people remember more after receiving instruction in remembering. I have already described (in Chapter 8) a number of investigations where children were instructed to follow plans or strategies customarily used by older individuals. You may recall, for example, that there were large improvements in children's memory when researchers gave rehearsal instructions to young children who did not rehearse spontaneously. As a rule, showing children how to use the strategies adopted by more mature individuals is highly effective. In numerous studies, doing so has led to large increases in recall.

Before I describe some projects designed to improve memory in older individuals, some points must be raised concerning the applicability of research findings to the ordinary circumstances of everyday life. If a demonstrated improvement is to be widely useful outside the psychological laboratory, it must be—at least potentially—long-lasting. However, although a number of studies have demonstrated that better remembering can be achieved, the improvement has not always been maintained. For example, when children are tested a week or so after the original session, they have sometimes stopped using a newly learned strategy, despite its effectiveness. As a result, memory performance decreases to the original level.

On the face of it, such a step backwards may appear surprising. One reflects, however, that even adults find new skills and new strategies difficult until they get into the habit of using them, and this takes time and practice. Until we have gained the habit of regularly using a new procedure it may be easier to continue with tried-and-true ways of doing things, however inefficient these may be. And although a new strategy may raise a child's level of performance, the benefits of the new strategy may seem insufficient to justify extra difficulty unless the task is one that the child perceives as having practical value in meeting her goals. The tendency to approach a task in the way that is most habitual and comfortable is especially strong if the experiment's circumstances appear to the individual to be strange and unfamiliar.

Whatever the precise reasons for children's failing to use a newly acquired memory strategy, it is clearly important to ensure that learned strategies are maintained if they are really to benefit the individual. In principle, there is no insuperable difficulty about this. It is simply necessary to make sure that a subject gets enough encouragement to practice using a new strategy, preferably in a variety of circumstances, and receives good feedback about its effectiveness. In these circumstances the new strategy will eventually become part of the individual's repertoire of habitual skills, and will be regularly used whenever the situation calls for it.

However beneficial a strategy is, its practical value will be small if it can only be used in situations that are identical to the one in which it was initially acquired. The individual must be able to *transfer* what has been learned to new circumstances. When intelligent adults are the learners, it is realistic to expect that the memory improvements psychologists observe will transfer to a variety of different tasks and circumstances. However, young children and people of low intellectual ability are not good at discerning different applicability of a skill. Nevertheless, it is likely that carefully designed training programs will be successful in extending the limited transfer typically exhibited by younger and less able people.

Instructional Procedures

Some particularly striking improvements in remembering have been observed in mentally retarded people. Individuals who are mentally retarded vary enormously, of course, but the majority of retarded people are very poor at remembering. Many important human skills necessitate information retention in memory; thus, retarded people are greatly handicapped by poor memory. Not surprisingly, psychologists have attempted to ascertain whether anything can be done to improve memory in retarded individuals. A number of instructional programs have been devised.

Some of the biggest successes at improving retarded people's memory have been achieved in a series of investigations by John Belmont and Earl Butterfield (1971; 1977; Butterfield, Wambold, & Belmont, 1973). These researchers with the view that the inferior remembering of retarded individuals is largely due to a failure to use effective strategies. Belmont and Butterfield thought that if retarded subjects were carefully trained to use good strategies, in particular ones customarily followed by people who remember well, performance would improve appreciably. To ensure that it would be possible to monitor the effects of teaching memory strategies to retarded learners, Belmont and Butterfield chose a particular memory task in which the effects of following a suitable strategy are usually large, and in which the extent to which subjects actually do engage in strategic behaviors is readily observed and measured.

In the chosen task, a list of letters is presented visually. The letters are exposed one at a time, in separate transparent windows on a black display panel. Subsequently, one of the items is shown again, on its own, and the subject has to point to the position on the panel where the letter first appeared. Belmont and Butterfield have used this procedure with sequences of varying length, up to eight letters. A number of the experiments involved adolescent subjects classified as moderately or mildly retarded. In the absence of training, the number of items these individuals recall correctly is around half that recalled by college students. For instance, when six-letter sequences are presented, retarded adolescents typically recall about 40% of the items, and college students recall more than 70%.

The investigators looked for differences in this memory task performance between normal and retarded subjects. Presentation of the single letters is usually self-paced. The first letter is exposed when the participant presses a button; the next letter appears (and the first one disappears) when the button is pressed again. Thus the rate at which letters appear is under the subject's control. Inspection of the records of normal adults' button pressing reveals that they do not expose each letter item for an equal amount of time. Typically, they follow a strategy of exposing the first few items fairly briefly, but after the third or fourth item they pause for considerably longer, in order to rehearse all the previous items as a group. They then press the button again to expose the next letter. A person who is given a six-letter list may expose each of the first three items, pause to rehearse (enabling them to become fairly consolidated in memory), and then rapidly expose each of the three final letters. The next step is to press the button exposing the "probe" letter, whose position in the list has to be identified (see Figure 9.1). When the probe letter appears, the typical adult strategy is to rapidly scan memory for the three most recent items. Because of their recency, these will probably still be available in memory. If the probe item is not located among them, the subject turns to the first three items. Since these have been carefully rehearsed, it is likely that they too are available in memory.

Only rarely do retarded adolescents spontaneously engage in this highly effective sequence of strategic activities. They typically run quickly through all six letters, without pausing to rehearse. Consequently, retarded subjects recall few letters correctly, and they are especially bad at remembering the letters near the beginning of a list. In the absence of adequate rehearsal these letters are soon forgotten.

In the research studies by Belmont and Butterfield, mentally retarded adolescents were taught to undertake the activities displayed by successful normal people. First, it was necessary to describe these activities in precise detail, making it possible to design an appropriate program of training. Figure 9.1 shows the sequence of actions taught. First, the participant exposes each of the first three letters, forming a group that is rehearsed together. Rehearsal of this group of letters ensures their recall, at least for a period of seconds. Next, the subject stops attending to the first three items and quickly exposes (but does not rehearse) each of the final three letters. These will remain temporarily available in memory for the very brief period of time required for the participant to expose the probe item and check whether it matches any of these final items. The person then presses the button to expose the probe letter. Participants quickly search through the unrehearsed final three letters, before they cease to be available in memory. If the probe item is identified among these final letters, the person simply reports its position. If the probe letter is *not* identified among the briefly available final items, he then inspects the remembered group of the first three letters. Since these

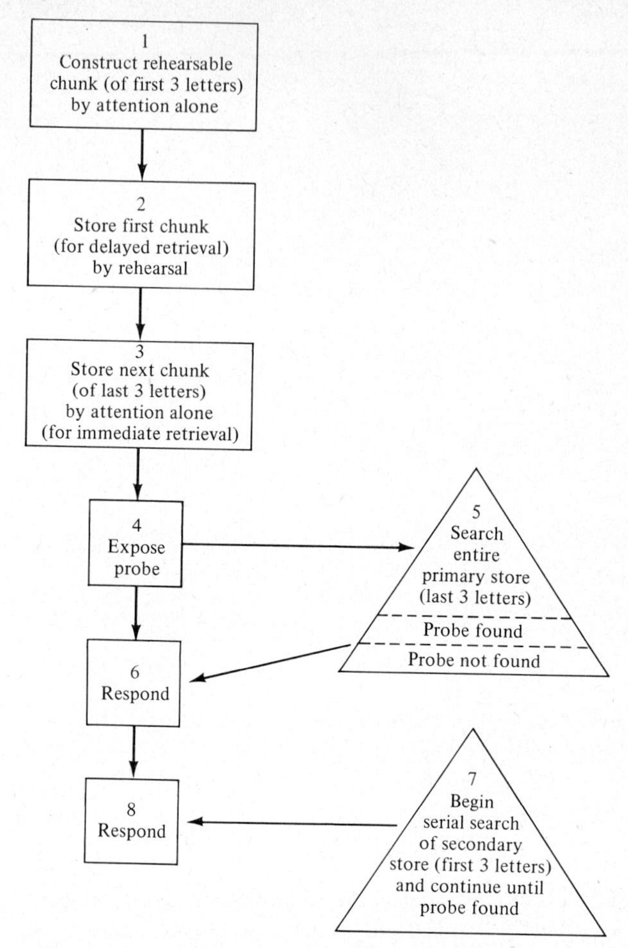

Figure 9.1 Sequence of steps taught to retarded adolescents by Butterfield, Wambold, and Belmont (1973).

letters have been rehearsed, they are not subject to such rapid decay as the later items. Finally, when the probe item is identified among the first three letters, the participant reports its position in the list.

The outcome of teaching retarded adolescents to perform all these activities in the proper sequence is shown in Figure 9.2. The line marked "Free" depicts recall in the absence of instructions. After training, the subjects achieved the much improved level of performance designated by "Acq 1." On a later session they were given a retention test (performance is designated by "Retent") and further training. This was followed, in a third session, by another test ("Acq 2"). Clearly, the training was highly successful; retarded participants' recall was greatly increased. The fact that near perfect performance was achieved indicates that re-

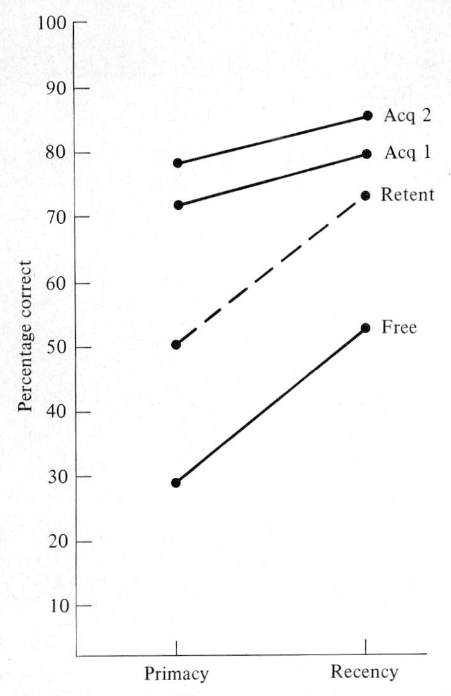

Figure 9.2 Effects of training on recall of early (*primary*) and late (*recency*) list items by retarded adolescents. *Source:* Butterfield, Wambold, and Belmont (1973).

tarded subjects did not lack any essential basic memory processes necessary for remembering the information. They simply could not, at the outset, control and coordinate the appropriate activities in a systematic, strategic plan. When they were carefully trained to do so, there was an immediate large improvement.

Another way to demonstrate the necessity of following a coordinated sequence of strategic activities is to get adults of normal intelligence to attempt a memory task in the same way that mentally retarded people do, abandoning the usual strategic activities. The findings of a number of investigations show that the outcome is depressed memory; the recall of normal people sinks to the very low performance levels usually found in mentally retarded subjects (Belmont, 1978).

The instructions provided by Belmont, Wambold, and Butterfield (1973) helped the retarded adolescent subjects by ensuring that materials were carefully rehearsed and efficiently retrieved. Other researchers found that remembering is improved by instructions to use alternative activities and strategies that contribute to the processing of items. For example, A. L. Brown and her colleagues (see Campione & Brown, 1977) have been very successful in helping mentally retarded subjects to improve their memory task performance. As in the case of Belmont's and Butterfield's work, the reasons for success lie in retarded people learning to undertake coordinated strategic activities.

Self-control of Memory Processes

It is encouraging to find that careful teaching produces large improvements in remembering. But, as I have already said, in order to make practical advances in skills important for human life, it is essential that the gains be maintained for lengthy periods, and that they transfer or generalize to tasks other than the somewhat artificial ones used in much psychological research. Belmont (1978) states that, for memory improvements to be really useful, a person does not just have to learn particular strategies, but must also be able to control and coordinate memory abilities. This aspect of metamemory is termed *self-programming* by Belmont, who makes an analogy between coordinating one's memory processes and programming a computer to control its own operation in order to achieve a goal. To program a computer to perform a task, it is necessary to know about the computer's basic operations. One must also know about the logic of programming. One must be able to devise programs, test them, locate errors, and rewrite a program until it works properly. Belmont notes that different jobs require different programs, and that programmers vary in skill. He continues:

> Likewise for memory skills. We have a job to do, and a brain that has many different information control processes and self-programming skills. As he practices doing a particular memory task, an able person will write himself a program, if you will. He will try this and that, evaluating his program as he goes along, and he will modify it until he has satisifed the job as he understands it to be. . . . Not surprisingly, people vary in their self-programming skills. (Belmont, 1978, p. 165)

Belmont lists a number of questions about memory improvement in retarded children. Under what conditions, he asks,

1. will retarded children's recall profit from direct instruction?
2. will they remember to use programs they have been taught?
3. will they generalize their training to new situations where it would be appropriate?
4. will they invent new programs?

As we have seen, the first of these possibilities definitely can take place when properly designed training is given. However, it is generally found that newly acquired memory skills are not maintained unless special care is given to the matter. There appears to be no insuperable problem: given adequate opportunities to practice memory skills and to become fully aware of their value, a child will continue to use newly taught plans and strategies. For instance, Brown, Campione, and Murphy (1977) found memory improvements produced by extensive training maintained for as long as a year. Finally, there is at present considerable uncertainty about the answers to Belmont's third and fourth questions.

IMPROVING OUR OWN REMEMBERING

Children and subnormal adults are not the only people who profit from remembering things better. We all do! There have been numerous descriptions in the previous chapters of procedures leading to memory improvements in intelligent students. In the final pages I will list, in summary form, some of the things students and others can do in order to achieve practical improvements in remembering.

1. In general, be aware that what you remember depends upon active processes that *you* undertake. It is up to you to process information in ways leading to distinctive and easily located memory traces of whatever you wish to remember. Keep in mind that your memory's achievements depend upon how it is cultivated, to use the garden plot analogy introduced in Chapter 1. Make sure you can use a range of effective memory strategies, and learn to select the strategic procedures that are most effective for the various demands upon your memory.

2. Realize the value of giving yourself ample rehearsal, repetition, and practice. Over short periods of time, small amounts of rehearsal can produce big differences in the extent that perceived information becomes fixed, or consolidated in memory (Chapter 2). When you rehearse, try to ensure that you are attending to the deeper meaning of the materials. Do not simply concentrate on physical aspects of the data, or consider each of a number of items in isolation from the others. The aim should be to continue and elaborate the meaningful information processing you are rehearsing, thereby giving yourself a better memory record: a more distinctive and more readily discriminate description of the information to be remembered. Rehearsal that simply maintains material in a superficially processed form has restricted value.

It is quite wrong to think that rehearsal and repetition are only used to remember meaningless or unstructured materials. The value of the kind of recitation where a person who is learning prose materials spends some of the study time in repeating the important content was demonstrated in a study by Gates (1917). Gates found that the amount of knowledge retained by adolescent (eighth grade) students after studying biographical information was greatly influenced by the relative proportions of time spent in reading and recitation. For example, those individuals who devoted 60% of their study time to recitation and the remainder to reading remembered 62% more information than students devoting all their study time to reading. The difference was even greater in younger children. Third grade students who spent 60% of their time reciting remembered twice as much of the biographical content as students who spent all the time reading. In Gates's experiments, the difference in remembering caused by varying the proportion of recitation time was nearly twice as great when retention was tested three to four hours after study than when a test was given immediately.

Clear implications follow from these and similar research findings. When you are reading something you wish to learn, spend a fair amount of time in running over the contents to yourself, in your own words. Active rehearsal is especially important when the content is difficult or unfamiliar. The more difficult the material, the more frequently you should stop to recite to yourself the meaningful content. By proceeding in this way you not only ensure that the information you need to remember is effectively processed, but you also help yourself to maintain close attention to the task. Consequently, you avoid falling into the not uncommon situation in which a student gradually becomes aware that for some time he has been failing to take in the full meaning of the passage being studied.

3. When you need to remember new and unfamiliar information, look for ways to connect or relate it to things you already know. A number of experiments described in Chapter 7 showed that people can use their existing knowledge in a number of ways to help learn new information. Most good teachers know the educational value of introducing metaphors: Typically, the aim is to make unfamiliar and abstract ideas more readily understandable by demonstrating their similarity to things already known and (usually) more concrete.

Sometimes, an unfamiliar prose passage can be made easier to understand and remember simply by giving it a descriptive title that directs the reader to that part of her own knowledge connected with the new materials (Chapter 7). Often meaning and structure are given to new information through existing knowledge schemas. The more you know about a particular area, the easier it is to remember related information. Experiments comparing good chess players with nonplayers in recalling chess piece positions provide clear demonstrations of this.

4. In addition to looking for connections between new information and things you already know, you can improve remembering by finding connections *within* materials. People are not at all good at remembering large numbers of entirely separate items: We can achieve much more if we find ways to relate each of a number of items to one another. The findings of Bower and Clark's experiment (1969) in which students made

up narratives to connect single words gave a good illustration of the memory improvements that can be achieved this way.

5. When a number of items cannot all be readily connected, it is often possible to increase recall by introducing an alternative form of organization. Sometimes this can be achieved by recoding items into a smaller number of distinct units; in other instances, grouping items into categories is possible. In Chapter 4, I described a number of ways of reorganizing materials to improve memory.

6. Make good use of verbal mnemonics when they are provided. One reason they are effective is their provision of ways to achieve the kinds of organization recommended in paragraphs 4 and 5 above. That is, mnemonics often make connections between separate items of information to be learned. Typically, a mnemonic technique may achieve this by forming a structured sentence from the first letter of each of a number of words (for example, "Richard Of York Gave Battle In Vain," for the colors of the rainbow) or by providing a rhyming verbal structure ("30 Days hath September. . . .").

7. Chapter 5 described some highly effective mnemonic systems dependent upon people's ability to make visual images. For example, the rhyme method ("One is a bun. . . ."), the link method and the method of loci, each of which requires the learner to make images of items to be remembered, are all highly effective for learning long lists.

8. Do not expect that the full value of a memory strategy must be apparent immediately, and avoid concluding that a technique is of no value if it does not produce immediate improvement. In a number of cases it has been shown that the long-term outcome of using a new strategy, compared with alternative methods, can be considerably better than any short-term advantage might suggest. For instance, in Bower and Clark's experiment (1969), students were asked to join items in word lists by forming connecting narratives. Immediate recall under this condition was no better than in a condition where students learned the same words by rote. Later, however, when students had looked at all the lists and were asked to recall again every item they could remember, those subjects who followed the narrative strategy remembered several times as many of the words than the other students. Another demonstration that the real value of a strategy may not be immediately apparent is given by the results of research by Gates mentioned in paragraph 2 above. Finally, note that the keyword method for foreign-language acquisition was also most successful, compared with alternative methods, after long periods of time. All these findings remind us that the immediate feedback we receive about the success of a recall strategy is by no means always a good guide to its real effectiveness.

9. There are some occasions when the wisest course is simply to ac-

cept our limited memory abilities, especially for short-term remembering of a number of separate items. We can look for ways to circumvent our memory limitations. We act in this way whenever we reach for pen and paper to solve a problem; we thereby transfer some of the information-retaining requirement of the task from our own memory system to an external store. Sometimes a task can be made easier by substituting a solution that makes light demands upon memory for one that requires greater remembering. An instance is the problem of discovering the idea of a right-angled triangle, when we only know the length of the baseline (b) and that of the hypotenuse (h). Miller (1956) notes that one solution is as follows:

(1) $h + b = v$
(2) $h - b = w$
(3) $v \times w = x$
(4) $\sqrt{x} = +y$
(5) $+y \times b = 2$
(6) $z/2 =$ area

The above solution is satisfactory, but it is highly inconvenient for learners because it is necessary to either remember all six steps or consult a written copy of the method every time it is to be used. Because of these difficulties, Miller calls the solution an "ugly" one, and contrasts it with an alternative method that achieves the same result without requiring as many steps. The alternative solution is as follows:

1. Find the altitude by the theory of Pythagoras.
2. Find the area of the triangle by multiplying base times altitude and dividing by two.

This second method is more convenient because it puts a smaller load upon one's memory for separate items of information. Note that it achieves this reduction by making more use of permanently stored knowledge. (Pythagorean theorem: The square of the hypotenuse is equal to the sum of the squares of the adjacent sides).

10. Finally, there are other factors that can influence remembering, although their effects on memory are less direct than those of the memory strategies, techniques, and processes emphasized throughout this book. One important indirect influence on remembering is attention: If you do not actually attend to the information you try to study, it is highly unlikely you will retain it. I have already drawn attention to the relationship between rehearsing and attention. Part of the value of certain study methods is due simply to their aiding attention. For instance, techniques such as note taking, and underlining important words in a book, can have the useful effect of helping a student attend to what he needs to know. In one study (Howe, 1970), when students took notes while listening to a

prose passage, they subsequently remembered over six times as much of their own notes' content (which they had no opportunity to inspect, since the notes were taken away immediately) as the other information in the passage. Doubtless a number of factors contributed to this result, but it is clear that differences in attention were crucially important.

References

Anderson, J. R. *Language, meaning and thought.* Hillsdale, N.J.: Erlbaum, 1976.

Anderson, R. C., Spiro, R. J., & Anderson, M. C. Schemata as scaffolding for the representation of information in connected discourse. *American Educational Research Journal,* 1978, *15,* 433–440.

Appel, L. F., Cooper, R. G., McCarrell, N., Sims-Knight, J., Yussen, S. R., & Flavell, J. H. The development of the distinction between perceiving and memorizing. *Child Development,* 1972, *43,* 1365–1381.

Atkinson, R. C. Mnemotechnics in second-language learning. *American Psychologist,* 1975, *30,* 821–828.

Atkinson, R. C., & Shiffrin, R. M. Human memory: A proposed system and its control processes. In K. Spence and J. T. Spence (Eds.), *The psychology of learning and motivation* (Volume 2). New York: Academic Press, 1968.

Atwood, M. E., & Polson, P. G. A process model for water jar problems. *Cognitive Psychology,* 1976, *8,* 191–216.

Baddeley, A. D. *The psychology of memory.* New York: Harper & Row, 1976.

Baddeley, A. D., Grant, S., Wight, E., & Thomson, N. Imagery and visual memory. In P. M. A. Rabbitt and S. Dornic (Eds.), *Attention and performance* (Volume 5). New York: Academic Press, 1974.

Baddeley, A. D., & Hitch, G. Working memory. In R. V. Kail & J. W. K. Hagan (Eds.), *Perspectives on the development of memory and cognition.* Hillsdale, N.J.: Erlbaum, 1974.

Bahrick, H. P., & Bahrick, P. O. A re-examination of the interrelations among measures of retention. *Quarterly Journal of Experimental Psychology,* 1964, *16,* 318–324.

Barclay, J. R., Bransford, J. D., Franks, J. J., McCarrell, N. S., & Nitsch, K. Comprehension and semantic flexibility. *Journal of Verbal Learning and Verbal Behavior,* 1974, *13,* 471–481.

Bartlett, F. C. *Remembering.* Cambridge, England: Cambridge University Press, 1932.

Belmont, J. M. Perceptual short-term memory in children, retardates and adults. *Journal of Experimental Child Psychology,* 1967, *5,* 114–122.

Belmont, J. M. Individual differences in memory: The cases of normal and retarded development. In M. M. Gruneberg & P. E. Morris (Eds.), *Aspects of memory.* London: Methuen, 1978.

Belmont, J. M., & Butterfield, E. C. Learning strategies as determinants of memory deficiencies. *Cognitive Psychology,* 1971, *2,* 236–248.

Belmont, J. M., & Butterfield, E. C. The instructional approach to developmental cognitive research. In R. V. Kail & J. W. Hagen (Eds.), *Perspectives on the development of memory and cognition.* Hillsdale, N.J.: Erlbaum, 1977.

Bousfield, W. A. The occurrence of clustering in the recall of randomly arranged associates. *Journal of General Psychology,* 1953, *49,* 229–240.

Bousfield, W. A., Cohen, B. H., & Whitmarsh, G. A. Associative clustering in the recall of words of different taxonomic frequencies of occurrence. *Psychological Reports,* 1958, *4,* 39–44.

Bower, G. H. Analysis of a mnemonic device. *American Scientist,* 1970, *58,* 496–510.

Bower, G. H. Mental imagery and associative learning. In L. W. Gregg (Ed.), *Cognition in learning and memory.* New York: Wiley, 1972.

Bower, G. H., & Clark, M. C. Narrative stories as mediators of serial learning. *Psychonomic Science,* 1969, *14,* 181–182.

Bower, G. H., Clark, M. C., Lesgold, A. M., & Winzenz, D. Hierarchical retrieval schemes in recall of categorised word lists. *Journal of Verbal Learning and Verbal Behavior,* 1969, *8,* 323–343.

Bransford, J. D. *Human cognition: Learning, understanding and remembering.* Belmont, Ca.: Wadsworth, 1979.

Bransford, J. D., & Franks, J. J. The abstraction of linguistic ideas. *Cognitive Psychology,* 1971, *2,* 331–350.

Bransford, J. D., & Johnson, M. K. Contextual prerequisites for understanding: Some investigations of comprehension and recall. *Journal of Verbal Learning and Verbal Behavior,* 1972, *11,* 717–726.

Bransford, J. D., & Johnson, M. K. Considerations of some problems of comprehension. In W. G. Chase (Ed.), *Visual information processing.* New York: Academic Press, 1973.

Broadbent, D. E. *Perception and communication.* Oxford: Pergamon, 1958.

Brown, A. L. Judgements of recency for long sequences of pictures: The absence of a developmental trend. *Journal of Experimental Child Psychology,* 1973, *15,* 437–480.

Brown, A. L. The development of memory: Knowing, knowing about knowing, and knowing how to know. In H. W. Reese (Ed.), *Advances in child development and behavior* (Volume 10). New York: Academic Press, 1975.

Brown, A. L., Campione, J. C., & Murphy, M. Keeping track of changing variables: long term retention of a trained rehearsal strategy by retarded adolescents. *American Journal of Mental Deficiency,* 1974, *78,* 446–453.

Brown, A. L., Smiley, S. S., Day, J. D., Townsend, M. A., & Lawton, S. C. Intrusion of a thematic idea in children's comprehension and retention of stories. *Child Development,* 1977, *48,* 1454–1466.

Brown, R., & McNeill, D. The "tip of the tongue" phenomenon. *Journal of Verbal Learning and Verbal Behavior,* 1966, *5,* 325–337.

Bruce, D., & Cofer, C. N. A comparison of recognition and recall in short-term memory. Proceedings of the 73rd Annual Convention, American Psychology Association, 1965, 81–82.

Bugelski, B. R., Kidd, E., & Segmen, J. Image as a mediator in one-trial paired-associate learning. *Journal of Experimental Psychology,* 1968, *76,* 69–73.

Butterfield, E. C., Wambold, C., & Belmont, J. M. On theory and practice of improving short-term memory. *American Journal of Mental Deficiency,* 1973, *77,* 654–669.

Campione, J. C., & Brown, A. L. Memory and metamemory development in educable retarded children. In R. V. Kail & J. W. Hagen (Eds.), *Perspectives on the development of memory and cognition.* Hillsdale, N.J.: Erlbaum, 1977.

Ceci, S. J., Caves, R. T., and Howe, M. J. A. Children's long-term memory for information that is incongruous with their prior knowledge. *British Journal of Psychology,* 1981, *72,* 443–450.

Ceci, S. J., & Howe, M. J. A. Semantic knowledge as a determinant of developmental differences in recall. *Journal of Experimental Child Psychology,* 1978a, *26,* 230–245.

Ceci, S. J., & Howe, M. J. A. Age-related differences in free recall as a function of retrieval flexibility. *Journal of Experimental Child Psychology,* 1978b, *26,* 432–442.

Cermak, L. S. *Human memory: Research and theory.* New York: Ronald Press, 1972.

Chi, M. T. H. Short-term limitations in children: Capacity or processing deficits? *Memory and Cognition,* 1976, *4,* 559–572.

Chi, M. T. H. Knowledge structures and memory development. In R. Siegler (Ed.), *Children's thinking: What develops?* Hillsdale, N.J.: Erlbaum, 1978.

Cofer, C. N. (Ed.). *The structure of human memory.* San Francisco: Freeman, 1975.

Collins, A. M., & Loftus, E. F. A spreading-activation theory of semantic processing. *Psychological Review,* 1975, *82,* 407–428.

Collins, A. M., & Quillian, M. R. Retrieval time from semantic memory. *Journal of Verbal Learning and Verbal Behavior,* 1969, *8,* 240–247.

Collins, A. M., & Quillian, M. R. How to make a language user. In E. Tulving and W. Donaldson (Eds.), *Organization of memory.* New York: Academic Press, 1972.

Coltheart, M., & Glick, M. J. Visual imagery: A case study. *Quarterly Journal of Experimental Psychology,* 1974, *24,* 55–65.

Conrad, C. Cognitive economy in semantic memory. *Journal of Experimental Psychology,* 1972, *92,* 149–154.

Conrad, R. An association between memory errors and errors due to acoustic masking of speech. *Nature,* 1962, *193,* 1314–1315.

Conrad, R. Acoustic confusions in immediate memory. *British Journal of Psychology,* 1964, *55,* 75–84.

Craik, F. I. M., & Lockhart, R. S. Levels of processing: A framework for memory research. *Journal of Verbal Learning and Verbal Behavior,* 1972, *11,* 671–684.

Craik, F. I. M., & Tulving E. Depth of processing and the retention of words in episodic memory. *Journal of Experimental Psychology: General,* 1975, *104,* 268–294.

Craik, F. I. M., & Watkins, M. J. The role of rehearsal in short-term memory. *Journal of Verbal Learning and Verbal Behavior,* 1973, *12,* 599–607.

Dale, H. C. A., & Baddeley, A. D. On the nature of alternatives used in testing recognition memory. *Nature,* 1962, *196,* 93–94.

Davis, R., Sutherland, N. S., & Judd, B. Information content in recognition and recall. *Journal of Experimental Psychology,* 1961, *61,* 422–428.

Epstein, W. The influence of syntactical structure on learning. *American Journal of Psychology,* 1961, *74,* 80–85.

Fagan, J. F. Infants' delayed recognition memory and forgetting. *Journal of Experimental Child Psychology,* 1973, *16,* 424–450.

Feldman, N. S., Klosson, E. C., Parsons, J. E., Rholes, W. S., & Ruble, D. N. Order of information presentation and children's moral judgments. *Child Development,* 1976, *21,* 490–506.

Flavell, J. H. *Cognitive development.* Englewood Cliffs, N.J.: Prentice-Hall, 1977.

Flavell, J. H., Beach, D. R., & Chinsky, J. M. Spontaneous verbal rehearsal in a memory task as a function of age. *Child Development,* 1966, *37,* 283–299.

Flavell, J. H., Friedrichs, A. G., & Hoyt, J. D. Developmental changes in memorization process. *Cognitive Psychology,* 1970, *1,* 324–340.

Flavell, J. H., & Wellman, H. M. Metamemory. In R. V. Kail & J. W. Hagen (Eds.), *Perspectives on the development of memory and cognition.* Hillsdale, N.J.: Erlbaum, 1977.

Gates, A. I. Recitation as a factor in memorizing. *Archives of Psychology,* 1917, *6,* whole no. 40.

Geis, M. F., & Hall, D. M. Encoding and congruity in children's incidental memory. *Child Development,* 1978, *49,* 857–861.

Geis, M. F., & Hall, D. Encoding and incidental memory in children. *Journal of Experimental Child Psychology,* 1976, *22,* 58–66.

Ghatala, E. S., Carbonari, J. P., & Bobele, L. Z. Developmental changes in incidental memory as a function of processing level, congruity, and repetition. *Journal of Experimental Child Psychology,* 1980, *29,* 74–87.

Glanzer, M., & Cunitz, A. R. Two storage mechanisms if in free recall. *Journal of Verbal Learning and Verbal Behavior,* 1966, *5,* 351–360.

Haber, R. N., & Haber, R. B. Eidetic imagery: 1. Frequency. *Perceptual and Motor Skills,* 1964, *19,* 131–138.

Hagen, J. W., & Stanovich, K. G. Memory: Strategies of acquisition. In R. V. Kail & J. W. Hagen (Eds.), *Perspectives on the development of memory and cognition.* Hillsdale, N.J.: Erlbaum, 1977.

Hart, J. T. Memory and the feeling-of-knowing experience. *Journal of Educational Psychology,* 1965, *56,* 208–216.

Hart, J. T. Second-try recall, recognition, and the memory-monitoring process. *Journal of Educational Psychology,* 1967, *58,* 193–197.

Holt, J. *How children fail.* New York: Pitman, 1964.

Howard, J. W., & Rothbart, M. Social categorization and memory for in-group and out-group behavior. *Journal of Personality and Social Psychology,* 1980, *38,* 301–310.

Howe, M. J. A. Consolidation in short-term memory as a function of rehearsal. *Psychonomic Science,* 1967a, *7,* 335–356.

Howe, M. J. A. Intra-list differences in short-term memory. Quarterly Journal of Experimental Psychology, 1965, *17,* 338–342.

Howe, M. J. A. Recognition memory for photographs in homogeneous sequences. *Perceptual and Motor Skills,* 1976b, *24,* 1181–1182.

Howe, M. J. A. Using students' notes to examine the role of the individual learner in acquiring meaningful subject matter. *Journal of Educational Research,* 1970, *64,* 61–63.

Hunter, I. M. L. An exceptional memory. *British Journal of Psychology,* 1977, *68,* 155–164.

Hunter, I. M. L. An exceptional talent for calculative thinking. *British Journal of Psychology,* 1962, *53,* 243–258.

Hunter, I. M. L. *Memory: Facts and fallacies* (2d ed.). Harmondsworth, England: Penguin, 1964.

Hunter, I. M. L. Memory in everyday life. In M. M. Grunebert & P. E. Morris (Eds.), *Applied problems in memory.* London: Academic Press, 1979.

Huttenlocher, J., & Burke, D. Why does memory span increase with age? *Cognitive Psychology,* 1976, *8,* 1–31.

Hyde, T. S., & Jenkins, J. J. Differential effects of incidental tasks on the organization of recall of a list of highly associated words. *Journal of Experimental Psychology,* 1969, *82,* 472–481.

Istomina, Z. M. The development of voluntary memory in pre-school age children. *Soviet Psychology,* 1975, *13,* 5–64.

Jacoby, L. L., Craik, F. I. M., & Begg, I. Effects or decision difficulty on recognition and recall. *Journal of Verbal Learning and Verbal Behavior,* 1979, *18,* 585–600.

Jahnke, J. C. Serial position effects in immediate serial recall. *Journal of Verbal Learning and Verbal Behavior,* 1963, 2, 284–287.

Jenkins, J. J., Mink, W. D., & Russell, W. A. Associate clustering as a function of verbal association strength. *Psychological Reports,* 1958, *4,* 127–136.

Jenkins, J. J., & Russell, W. A. Associative clustering during recall. *Journal of Abnormal and Social Psychology,* 1952, *47,* 818–821.

Jensen, A. R. *Educability and group differences.* New York: Harper & Row, 1973.

Jensen, A. R., & Rohwer, W. D. Verbal mediation in paired-associate and serial learning. *Journal of Verbal Behavior,* 1963, *1,* 346–351.

Kail, R. V. *The development of memory in children.* San Francisco: Freeman, 1979.

Keeney, T. J., Cannizzo, S. R., & Flavell, J. H. Spontaneous and induced verbal rehearsal in a recall task. *Child Development,* 1967, *38,* 953–966.

Kingsley, P. R., & Hagen, J. W. Induced versus spontaneous rehearsal in short-term memory in nursery school children. *Developmental Psychology,* 1969, *1,* 40–46.

Kintsch, W. Memory for prose. In C. N. Cofer (Ed.), *The structure of human memory.* San Francisco: Freeman, 1975.

Kintsch, W. *Memory and cognition.* New York: Wiley, 1972.

Kintsch, W., & Buschke, H. Homophones and synonyms in short-term memory. *Journal of Experimental Psychology,* 1969, *80,* 403–407.

Kobasigawa, A. Utilization of retrieval cues by children in recall. *Child Development,* 1974, *45,* 127–134.

Kreutzer, M. A., Leonard, C., & Flavell, J. H. An interview study of children's knowledge about memory. *Monographs of the Society for Research in Child Development,* 1975, 40 (1, Serial no. 159).

Light, L., & Carter-Sobell, L. Effects of changed semantic context on recognition memory. *Journal of Verbal Learning and Verbal Behavior,* 1970, *9,* 1–11.

Loftus, E. F., & Palmer, J. C. Reconstruction of automobile destruction: An example of the interaction between language and memory. *Journal of Verbal Learning and Verbal Behavior,* 1974, *13,* 585–589.

Luria, A. R. *The mind of a mnemonist.* New York: Basic Books, 1968.

McNulty, J. A. A partial learning model of recognition memory. *Canadian Journal of Psychology,* 1966, *20,* 302–315.

Mandler, G. Organisation and memory. In K. W. Spence & J. T. Spence (Eds.), *The psychology of learning and motivation* (Volume 2). New York: Academic Press, 1968.

Mandler, G., & Pearlstone, Z. Free and constrained concept learning and subsequent recall. *Journal of Verbal Learning and Verbal Behavior,* 1966, *5,* 126–131.

Mandler, G., Pearlstone, Z., & Koopmans, H. S. Effects of organization and semantic similarity on a recall and recognition task. *Journal of Verbal Learning and Verbal Behavior,* 1969, *8,* 410–423.

Marks, L. E., & Miller, G. A. The role of semantic and syntactic constraints in the memorization of English sentences. *Journal of Verbal Learning and Verbal Behavior,* 1964, *3,* 1–5.

Miller, G. A. Information and memory. *Scientific American,* August, 1956.

Miller, G. A., & Selfridge, J. A. Verbal context and the recall of meaningful material. *American Journal of Psychology,* 1950, *63,* 176–185.

Minsky, M. A framework for representing knowledge. In P. H. Winston (Ed.), *The psychology of computer vision.* New York: McGraw-Hill, 1975.

Moely, B. E. Production deficiency in young children's clustered recall. *Developmental Psychology,* 1969, *1,* 26–34.

Moynahan, E. D. The development of knowledge concerning the effect of categorization upon free recall. *Child Development,* 1973, *44,* 238–246.

Nelson, T. O. Repetition and depth of processing. *Journal of Verbal Learning and Verbal Behavior,* 1977, *16,* 151–171.

Noble, C. E. An analysis of meaning. *Psychological Review,* 1952, *59,* 421–430.

Norman, D. A., & Rumelhart, D. E. *Explorations in cognition.* San Francisco: Freeman, 1975.

Novinski, L. S. A re-examination of the part-whole effect in free recall. *Journal of Verbal Learning and Verbal Behavior,* 1972, *11,* 228–233.

Ornstein, P. A., Naus, M. J., and Liberty, C. Rehearsal and organizational processes in children's memory. *Child Development,* 1975, *46,* 818–830.

Paivio, A. Abstractness, imagery, and meaningfulness in paired-associate learning. *Journal of Verbal Learning and Verbal Behavior*, 1965, *4*, 32–38.

Paivio, A. Paired-associate learning and free recall of nouns as a function of concreteness specificity, imagery, and meaningfulness. *Psychological Reports*, 1967, *20*, 239–245.

Paivio, A. Mental imagery in associative learning and memory. *Psychological Review*, 1969, *76*, 241–263.

Paivio, A., Yuille, J. C., & Rogers, T. B. Noun imagery and meaningfulness in free and serial recall. *Journal of Experimental Psychology*, 1969, *79*, 509–514.

Patterson, K. E. Some characteristics of retrieval limitation in long-term memory. *Journal of Verbal Learning and Verbal Behavior*, 1972, *11*, 685–691.

Peterson, L. R., & Peterson, M. J. Short-term retention of individual verbal terms. *Journal of Experimental Psychology*, 1959, *58*, 193–198.

Pichert, J. W., & Anderson, R. C. Taking different perspectives on a story. *Journal of Educational Psychology*, 1977, *69*, 309–315.

Pressley, G. M. Children's use of the keyword method to learn simple Spanish vocabulary words. *Journal of Educational Psychology*, 1977, *69*, 465–472.

Pylyshyn, Z. W. What the mind's eye tells the mind's brain: A critique of mental imagery. *Psychological Bulletin*, 1973, *80*, 1–24.

Raugh, M. R., & Atkinson, R. C. A mnemonic method for learning a second language vocabulary. *Journal of Educational Psychology*, 1975, *67*, 1–16.

Raugh, M. R., Schupbach, R. D., & Atkinson, R. C. Teaching a large Russian language vocabulary by the mnemonic keyword method. *Instructional Science*, 1977, *6*, 199–221.

Reder, L. M., Anderson, J. R., & Bjork, R. A. A semantic interpretation of encoding specificity. *Journal of Experimental Psychology*, 1974, *102*, 648–656.

Rips, L. J., Shoben, E. J., & Smith, E. E. Semantic distance and the verification of semantic relations. *Journal of Verbal Learning and Verbal Behavior*, 1973, *12*, 1–20.

Roberts, W. A. The priority of recall of new items in transfer from part-list learning to whole-list learning. *Journal of Verbal Learning and Verbal Behavior*, 1969, *8*, 465–562.

Rogers, T. B., Kuiper, N. A., & Kirker, W. S. Self-references and the encoding of personal information. *Journal of Personality and Social Psychology*, 1977, *35*, 677–688.

Rogoff, B., Newcombe, N., & Kagan, J. Planfulness and recognition memory. *Child Development*, 1974, *45*, 972–977.

Ross, J., & Lawrence, K. A. Some observations on memory artifice. *Psychonomic Science*, 1968, *13*, 107–108.

Rundus, D. Analysis of rehearsal processes in free recall. *Journal of Experimental Psychology*, 1971, *80*, 63–77.

Schank, R. C., & Abelson, R. P. *Scripts, plans, goals and understanding: An inquiry into human knowledge structures.* Hillsdale, N.J.: Erlbaum, 1977.

Segal, S. J., & Fusella, V. Effects of imaging on signal-to-noise ratio with varying signal conditions. *British Journal of Psychology*, 1969, *60*, 459–464.

Shepard, R. N. Recognition memory for words, sentences and pictures. *Journal of Verbal Learning and Verbal Behavior*, 1967, *6*, 156–163.

Slamecka, N. J., Moore, T., & Carey, S. Part-to-whole transfer and its relation to organisation theory. *Journal of Verbal Learning and Verbal Behavior*, 1972, *11*, 73–82.

Smith, E. E. Theories of semantic memory. In W. K. Estes (Ed.), *Handbook of learning and cognitive processes* (Volume 6). Hillsdale, N.J.: Erlbaum, 1978.

Snyder, M., & Uranowitz, S. W. Reconstructing the past: Some cognitive consequences of person perception. *Journal of Personality and Social Psychology*, 1978, *36*, 940–950.

Spear, J. R., & Flavell, J. H. Young children's knowledge of the relative difficulty of recognition and recall memory tasks. Unpublished paper, Stanford University, 1977.

Sperling, G. A model for visual memory tasks. *Human Factors 5*, 1963, 19–31.

Spiro, R. J. Accomodative reconstruction in prose recall. *Journal of Verbal Learning and Verbal Behavior*, 1980, *19*, 84–95.

Standing, L., Conezio, J., & Haber, R. N. Perception and memory for pictures: Single-trial learning of 2560 visual stimuli. *Psychonomic Science*, 1970, *19*, 73–74.

Stevenson, H. W., Parker, T., & Wilkinson, A. Ratings and measures of memory processes in young children. Unpublished manuscript, University of Michigan, 1975.

Tresselt, M. E., & Mayzner, M. S. A study of incidental learning. *Journal of Psychology*, 1960, *60*, 339–347.

Tulving, E. Subjective organization and effects of repetition in multi-trial free-recall learning. *Journal of Verbal Learning and Verbal Behavior*, 1966, *5*, 193–197.

Tulving, E. Subjective organization in free-recall of unrelated words. *Psychological Review*, 1962, *69*, 344–354.

Tulving, E., & Osler, S. Effectiveness of retrieval cues in memory for words. *Journal of Experimental Psychology*, 1968, *77*, 593–601.

Tulving, E., and Pearlstone, Z. Availability versus accessibility of information in memory for words. *Journal of Verbal Learning and Verbal Behavior*, 1966, *5*, 381–391.

Tulving, E., and Thomson, D. M. Encoding specificity and retrieval processes in episodic memory. *Psychological Review*, 1973, *80*, 352–373.

Tulving, E., and Watkins, M. J. Structure of memory traces. *Psychological Review*, 1975, *82*, 261–275.

Turnure, J., Buium, N., and Thurlow, M. The effectiveness of interrogatives for promoting verbal elaboration productivity in young children. *Child Development*, 1976, *47*, 851–855.

Wellman, H. M., Ritter, K., and Flavell, J. H. Deliberate memory behavior in the delayed reactions of very young children. *Developmental Psychology*, 1975, *11*, 780–787.

Wood, G., and Clark, D. Instruction, ordering and previous practice in free-recall learning. *Psychonomic Science*, 1969, *14*, 187–188.

Yussen, S. R., and Levy, V. M. Developmental changes in predicting one's own span of short-term memory. *Journal of Experimental Child Psychology*, 1975, *19*, 502–508.

Index

83 84 85 9 8 7 6 5 4 3 2 1